MAGGIE
A Lifelong MG Love Affair

Tom McCooey

Scratching Shed Publishing Ltd

Copyright © Tom McCooey 2024
All rights reserved
The moral right of the authors has been asserted
First published by Scratching Shed Publishing Ltd in 2024
Registered in England & Wales No. 6588772
Registered office: 47 Street Lane, Leeds, West Yorkshire. LS8 1AP
www.scratchingshedpublishing.co.uk
ISBN: 978-1068618970

Cover: Will McCooey in Southport, early 1980s; Tom, aged five, with the MGs at his childhood home; Maggie pictured at Carr Hill, near St Helens.
Back cover (clockwise): Maggie on the road; Tom flummoxed over the bonnet of the stricken Magnette; Out for a drive after the ZA was back on the road; Pete Brierley tries the starting handle to unseize the engine prior to restoration.
All images © Tom McCooey

No part of this book may be reproduced or transmitted in any form or by any other means without the written permission of the publisher, except by a reviewer who wishes to quote brief passages in connection with a review written for insertion in a magazine, newspaper or broadcast.

Every effort has been made to obtain the necessary permissions with reference to copyright material, both illustrative and quoted. We apologise for any omissions in this respect and will be pleased to make the appropriate acknowledgements in any future edition.

A catalogue record for this book is available from the British Library.

Printed and bound in the UK by

Unit 600, Fareham Reach, Fareham Road
Gosport, Hampshire, PO13 0FW

For Sharon and Sophie.
Because of Will.

'Tom's resurrection of an MG that's been in his family for generations is a story that should inspire all budding classic car nuts. His enthusiasm for Maggie shines through the many highs and lows of this huge undertaking, which he writes about with a deft honesty that chronicles the many challenges of a first-time resto. It's a delight to see this wonderful piece of Fifties history firmly back on the road, where it belongs.'

DAVID SIMISTER
EDITOR, *CLASSIC CAR WEEKLY*

Contents

1. A Cold Night in January 1
2. Why is There a Taxi in Your Garage? 9
3. Montego Man 18
4. The First Resurrection...24
5. Maggie's First Attempt...30
6. Progress Stalled 34
7. My Own Wheels 41
8. Driving Up the Wall 49
9. Starting Over 54
10. A (big) Bump in the Road 63
11. Plan MGB 78
12. Midgeteering 84
13. Coming Home..91
14. It Begins 99
15. The Appraisal 114
16. Cap in Hand 132
17. Admitting Defeat 140
18. A Wedding, Without the Car 144
19. Another Bump in the Road 156
20. Lockdown 168
21. Car Fanatics Mark III 181
22. Two-Brew Job...196
23. On With the Show 211
24. The Past 218
25. The Future..227
26. Afterword 235
    Acknowledgements 239

Foreword

*By Dominic Taylor-Lane
– Founder and MD of
The Association of Heritage Engineers*

'I helped design the suspension on these with Gerald Palmer,' said Peter, my late father-in-law, as we winched what is now my '57 Magnette ZB Varitone, 94 LMH out of her then 'final' resting place deep in the Devonshire countryside. Imaginatively painted black from new and registered in South London, it allegedly had 'Goodwood history' (it might have been there on occasion, but I doubt it was further than the car park...)

I then went to work in Scotland for three years. On my return the car was 50 per cent complete, just one of Peter's 'retirement projects'. Sadly, Peter left us before it was finished but, determined to see the project to completion, I purchased it from the family, technically finished it myself, and from that day drove it at every opportunity. Nowadays, myself and my sons drive it 'vigorously'. So we have three generations of Magneteers in the family.

Classic cars are so evocative, family cars in particular. Whilst often illogical and on occasion infuriating, they make memories, initiate stories and illicit smiles during and after custodianship.

Tom's car 'journey' through these pages exemplifies just how they can conjure up a time, a place, an experience, an emotion.

It has been 11 years since I first took 'Lady Margaret' out of the garage to attend her first Silverstone festival with the MG car club line-up, 18 years after Peter first started the project. It also happens to be the longest I have owned any car from the 60 or so I've had, which might tell you what it means to me.

My Magnette isn't what you would call an original specification but it was always Peter's intention to make it as drivable and safe in modern road conditions as possible. More power, better brakes, more comprehensive wiring and, above all, greater comfort were its starting points.

I have developed the car in my ownership and, like Tom, I want it to be used for as long as possible. My work with companies producing sustainable liquid fuels suggest that the 'solution' is exactly that. If you can take a car whose manufacturing 'carbon footprint' was paid back many decades ago, and use a sustainable fuel to power it, then you have one of the most sustainable means of conveyance and leisure in existence.

I never thought I would fall for an MG Magnette. Before I met Peter I didn't know they even existed. But like him, and many others, I have found it to be one of the best all-round classic sporting saloons of its era and beyond. From Goodwood to Le Mans, from Oxford to Angoulême, it has never let me down or left me disappointed.

Tom's experiences and story mirror so many of my own; one of the many reasons his narrative is so compelling.

Dominic Taylor-Lane
September 2024

Maggie with the author's mum and dad on their wedding day, March 1983

*'Life is like a petrol pump.
It's a gas.'*
— **Will McCooey**

A Cold Night in January

MG Magnette ZA
Top speed: 79.7 mph
0-60: 23.1 seconds
Economy: 24.9 mpg
Cost when new: £914 including taxes

I swung off the garage door, resting my forehead on the back of my hands as I held the bottom of it. It made that really satisfying swooshing noise before the metallic clink and the sudden stop to my forward lurch told me the end of the rail had been found.

My hands were cold. I was putting out the bins and it was one of those nights that started before work ended and promised little more than shite telly with your tea — the ones after Christmas but not so close to the festivities that you are filled with the energy brought by the promise you made to yourself at New Year.

The dim light in the garage was a reminder that I needed something better than the energy saving bulb that is still there. Maybe a putting strip light in is a job I ought to have done during lockdown.

This was long before that though — it was the middle of January 2018, and trips to the garage at this point in time were not enjoyable. Our growing collection of bins lined the front, and further inside was a jumble of stuff belonging to the back garden kept out of harm's way over winter, as well as boxes intended for the loft once I'd got around to getting it boarded. There was no hope of squeezing around to the shelves at the back to access the tools to do jobs in the house which were on hold, such as putting up shelves and hanging pictures and, in the middle of all this mess, was the vehicle that was slowly becoming a big regret. The feeling was consuming me much in the way the rust had slowly eaten away at the car through all the years before.

Staring at me from behind the bins, into which I had loudly deposited empty cans of chopped tomatoes after retrieving them from the ground, was my MG. It sounds ridiculous but there is a sort of human quality in its headlamps when it is just sitting there, and the eye contact it manages to make in circumstances such as these might remind you, if you are as inclined to attach sentiment to inanimate objects as I am, of a puppy about to be taken to the vet. I blame being brought up on books like *The Little Red Metro*. Meet Maggie.

As far as classic cars go, this one isn't particularly desirable. It's a 1956 MG Magnette, series ZA, to give its proper name. Maggie, as you have already sussed, is a common and not-so imagainitve shortening of Magnette. They aren't worth a great deal when compared to other cars which may look vaguely similar, such as a Jaguar MKII. They don't go very fast and at that moment mine was essentially about a third of a complete car.

That encourages a very valid question — the type of question which prompts a hand carrying a pint towards a pair of expectant lips to pause mid-flight, while the operator ponders it and can only come out with an erm-ridden — 'it's a long story.' And it is. As the imaginary pint clunks on the table, the plainest way of explaining the predicament that remained in the garage once I'd closed the door, and plagued my mind that evening (long after also pondering it while cooking the pot of chilli those tomatoes contributed to) is that it is a grief project. There's an argument — a valid one — to say my addiction to classic cars is a way of dealing with grief.

My car once belonged to my dad. Very kindly, mum agreed I could have it when he died, perhaps because she knew I was the only one daft enough to try and do anything with it rather than let it sit in her garage — not deteriorating, but definitely not getting any better.

But SLC 620, or 'Maggie' as dad called it/her, was not just his car. Calling it his pride and joy would be an understatement despite the fact it hadn't turned a wheel during my entire lifetime, which stood at 32-and-two-thirds when I had my first go at writing this book in 2020. In reality, dad was unrivalled in his passion for many things and we were lucky that those things included me, my brothers, sister and mum. But they also stretched to discount book shops, cooking spaghetti Bolognese in his shirt and underpants (so his work trousers didn't absorb the cooking smell), the music of American singer-songwriter and guitarist Richie Havens (1941-2013), vintage buses and the routes they took around St Helens and... well, you get the idea. Underpinning all that though, the banner picture at the top of life's Facebook page was Maggie. It even served as my parents' wedding car on 25th March, 1983.

The problem for my dad came later. Running classic cars and having kids don't always mix (they never mix, actually), and when both demand being plugged into your financial resources, those parents of my dad's inclination (which you'd hope is most) prioritise their offspring. From what I can gather, a few intended months off the road because of a minor issue turned into years as children numbers two, three and four came along to scupper any plans of vehicular resurrection. It's not just having children either, there are lots of reasons why pressing 'SORN' on the

DVLA's website can spell doom for an old motor.

Maggie's story in this family begins in 1982 when a friend of dad's bought her and promptly had to sell her again because his wife wasn't a fan (so the story goes). My dad had been introduced to the car shortly after his friend's acquisition of it, and at a guess the conversation would have gone something like:

'Wow! That's a lovely car.' (That's dad speaking).
'I know, it's a shame I have to sell it.'
'What? Why? You've only just bought it.'
'Mrs doesn't like it...'
'Oh, well I'll have it then.'

What actually happened after that is my dad's dad paid the friend £675 for Maggie plus a further £10 for the handbook, which I know because I have the receipt in a tatty envelope slid inside the front cover of said publication.

On the bottom of the receipt, in my granddad's enviably eloquent handwriting, it reads: 'Transferred to William 29th April 1982,' which would have made Maggie his 27th birthday present.'

So, when you think about it, the reason I closed the garage door, with a freezing hand, on a view that has more than once put me in a shitty mood is because one of my dad's friends would rather not have upset his wife 36 years before.

While it is fair to say that if you own one of these cars the likelihood is you won't see another on a trip to the shops, it is also fair to say that in classic car terms they aren't an outward sign of wealth, appreciation of performance or status.

The Z-types are split into three models, four if you include the later BMC Farina, which carried a Magnette badge but would leave people staring at a family photo of them wondering if the milkman had anything to do with it.

These are the ZA, ZB and ZB Varitone, which all look similar, save for a few minor variations. Each has their own specs and fan clubs, probably depending on what other people's dads bought from their friends whose wives didn't like them.

There are other books all about the technical specifications of Z-types and if you're interested in that you'll have already read them. This isn't that sort of book or really a book about a single car at all — it's about a car representing a life story. It's about growing-up, peeing on the verge of the road, peeing in the car, holding the steering wheel of a moving Montego, aged five, and being terrified, before fish and chips in the back of said Montego when it broke down. Then there was sitting in a bin bag after rugby training so my dad's BMW didn't get muddy and learning to drive in one of the most embarrassing vehicles ever made.

Cars followed me into bands ... playing with Bon Jovi ... a wedding ... a divorce ... starting again ... new jobs ... the deaths of family members ... another wedding ... going back to school ... coronavirus ... a baby ... make that two babies.

Underpinning all of that is Maggie. She's always been there, waiting her turn after each false start.

This car that I had never seen move under its own steam for the longest time means an awful lot. Old it may be, but it's also about being seven-years-old and standing in my parents' garage, which feelings flood back whenever I smell the leather interior. It's restoring my dad's pride and joy. It's my tribute to his memory.

The new MG Magnette was shown to the world in October 1953 at the London Motor Show at Earls Court. Designed by Gerald Palmer, the ZA was the first MG with a monocoque chassis (the structure is integral with the body) and it was marketed as 'airsmoothed', which put some distance between it and the boxy pre-war designs a lot of car manufacturers had continued to build when their factories were running again. It also divided opinion.

Apart from the look of horror enthusiasts would have greeted the dummy radiator cap with, the merger of Morris and Austin to create the British Motor Corporation saw 'badge engineered' cars appear on forecourts, though in reality the only things the ZA shared with the similar Wolsley 4/44 were its roof and boot lid.

MG had also aimed the Magnette at a specific section of the car-buying market. As a luxury sports saloon, its leather upholstery, plush carpets and heater as standard aimed it squarely at bank managers and the like, though you had to pay extra for a radio. It's a pretty accurate assumption by the makers of *Call the Midwife* that Dr Turner drives one. His is a lovely green one registered in 1957, beautifully patinated but with flashing indicators instead of semaphores. The ZB had replaced the ZA by then, so we will assume this one was built in '56 before its registration the following March.

A quick check on the DVLA website tells me it's currently on SORN but that's no need to panic. Anyway, that's me on a tangent — it happens when you start Googling cars.

At £914 after taxes, the ZA cost almost twice the average 1953 yearly wage of £481 and considering houses cost about £2,750 on average, it would be fair to assume you were going places. Literally, if you were seen in a Magnette. Alongside the Wolseley, it was seen as a driver's car and 'sporting' saloon, so the absence of a rev counter does seem odd.

Under the big bonnet, which has since caused countless bleeds to the head, was a four-cylinder 1,489cc B-Series engine and under the driver's right foot was a manageable 60bhp, which could reach 80mph — not something a driver of 21st-century tuition would want to do, mind, in a car with no seatbelts.

To cut a long history short, the ZA was replaced by the more powerful, but aesthetically nearly the same ZB in 1956. There was also a Varitone model, which was similar to the ZB but had a larger back window and usually came with a two-tone paint job, hence the name.

The MkIII introduced in 1959 wasn't a Magnette at all but a

Pinin Farina-designed midsize BMC, which was also badged as an Austin A55 Cambridge Mark II, Morris Oxford V and Wolseley 15/60.

Of the ZA, B and Varitone, 36,601 were made, and about 800 or so are thought to survive. A big factor in a sharp drop in numbers in the '70s is down to stricter regulations in the MOT test. Despite having a strong overall structure, the Z-types were – and still are – prone to rot and, in 1977, along with checks of windscreen wipers and washers, indicators, brake lights, horns and the exhaust system, the tester was henceforth asked to assess the condition of the body structure and chassis.

When introduced in 1960, the MOT only covered brakes, lights and steering and was only required for cars that were ten years old, plus every year after that. A tyre check was introduced in 1968 before the more stringent requirements from '77. And surviving Z-types, the youngest being 18 years old at this point, didn't tend to fare too well under the tester's hammer.

Metalwork is costly and by then a tatty Z-type could be bought for about £50, meaning there was no point in putting effort into decent repairs.

Many models were subsequently swept-up by those with a taste for banger racing, an activity which makes many classic car enthusiasts wince. There's a lot more to it, but the basic idea is cars seen to be beyond repair were throttled around circuits like Wimbledon greyhound track in races where contact was not only allowed but encouraged, with some events requiring the winner to be the 'last car standing.'

There will always be arguments about banger racing as long as there are cars, but I was lucky — or not, depending on how you view the situation in my garage — that Maggie avoided this fate and thus was around to blow a medium-sized house deposit-sized hole into my finances.

The day that January cold made my fingertips on the garage door feel brittle, I had received an invoice from the company doing the metalwork on the car which was a little larger than was welcome, so much so I had to call my mum — at the age of 30 — with my best cap-in-hand voice to borrow a chunk of money that still hasn't been paid back.

The envelope the bill came in was thick and slightly ripped along the bottom where the rain had caught it between the postbag and my letterbox. I knew from the weight that there would be a decent itemised list of how each of my hours at £35 plus VAT was spent.

My mum has never been a person I have been afraid of, but when I put my foot in it I still get that lump in my throat as I plot how to tell her things like I was the last one to see the cat run up the garden before it went missing, or how to ask for £6,384.84 three weeks after Christmas when I knew full-well she had wanted a new bathroom for five years. It's the sort of call you start by asking, 'Am I on speaker?' in case a sibling hears what you're about to say. I suppose this is also a test to see if they ever read what I write.

To make matters worse, that was when the original budget for bringing the car back on the road was bust — hence my appeal to my mum and my heavy heart.

As the garage door clunked shut and the key made an echoey scraping sound I had two options that kept me awake that night. Give up and sell the car, at the cost of maybe a lifetime's worth of regret and for a lot less than I'd already spent on it, or stick at it and endure however much longer was in front of both of us.

My heart had made the decision before I'd even made it back inside the house, but my paperwork tells me it took me until the following May for my head to catch up.

Why is There a Taxi in Your Garage?

Austin FX4

If you don't like cars, or don't know very much about MG Z-types, and then you squinted and looked at an Austin FX4 i.e. a black taxi cab, you could maybe be forgiven for confusing them. Basically, a black ZA shares its colour with a black cab, has slightly rounded features, a longish bonnet and a big grille. But they still don't look alike. Unless you are among the people who'd ask my dad. Every. Single. Time.

The question was a frequent one throughout my childhood. If friends were ever round and the garage door was open, it wasn't a case of *if* they would ask, but *when*.

Looking at Maggie, you can sort of, maybe, see some sort of resemblance to a Hackney carriage, especially because she is painted black. If you picture a Hackney cab in your mind you probably don't know it but you'll be imagining an Austin FX4. It has round headlamps, distinctive rounded front wings, a big front grille and is black. Interestingly, that was also a BMC car and introduced in 1958 — a good while after the Z-types.

Anyway.

Throughout my childhood there were two constants: home and the cars in my parents' garage, both MGs.

Friends were always more impressed with Mum's MG Midget. It was a 1500 model, of the type that purists would turn their nose up at if they were to see it at a show nowadays.

There were many incarnations of the Midget before this, but for ease of understanding we'll start in 1961 with the MKI and the shape people would recognise as a Midget (or Austin Healey Sprite — there's that badge engineering again).

By the time the MKIV was launched in 1974, or 1500 as it was known, the A-series engine had been replaced with the 1493cc block from the Triumph Spitfire, and it looked very different to the enthusiast. Big plastic bumpers, known as rubber bumpers, to meet US regulations had been added, as well as an increased ride height by six inches. This affected the handling and necessitated anti-roll bars and the engine, which was too big for the car really, had a habit of over-heating.

There are many problems with the MKIV, not helped by the fiasco affecting British Leyland at the time, about which there is also plenty of other reading available written by people better qualified to explain it than myself. But to my parents this car had sentimental value. To me and other kids in primary school who didn't know any better, it just looked cool.

The Midget is known as JED, because that's his, yes *his*, registration plate. He is the 58th from the last ever Midget built, and was completed on Monday 3rd December, 1979. The last ever Midget was finished on the Friday. That is EOL 733V and is at the British Motor Museum in Warwick, in case you were wondering. It's fitting the reg reads EOL, which I like to think stands for 'End of Line'.

The last 500 Midgets were painted black, making both MGs

in our garage the same colour, and that affliction every member of my childhood household suffers from — attaching sentiment to inanimate objects — was made worse by my dad proposing to my mum in theirs.

Before I was born there was another Midget belonging to my dad. That was also a 1500, built in 1976, and it too was painted black as a special order. Its registration is NTB 300R and I still have some of my dad's tax discs for it.

This rather neatly brings me onto looking-up old cars on the DVLA website. By typing in the registration number you can find very simple details such as make of car, date of registration and a few other details. Importantly, you can see if the car has current tax and MOT, and the dates are shown in a reassuring pastel green box. A dreaded 'rex box' with a white cross means the car is either in a garage or under a tarpaulin on a drive somewhere with grass growing around the tyres, or that it has met its fate at the scrapyard. Of course, you probably know that already, and a lot of you will have done the same.

My dad would, when I was younger, scour forums and the 'lost and found' sections of websites and magazines looking for NTB. After his death I started doing likewise with any car I could remember the reg of or could find a picture of to remind me.

My grandad's old Escort that a man bought to restore in the late '90s is on a SORN, a sign it's not – or at least shouldn't be – on the road but maybe still alive, resting in a garage somewhere. The Montego that ferried me to rugby matches in far-flung Sunday-morning destinations such as Saddleworth when I was a kid – untaxed, unMOT-ed, presumed dead.

I typed in NTB 300R. No tax. Bugger. But encouragingly the car did have an MOT — maybe it was having a rest for a while, or maybe it was for sale?

A few months later, and after another check on the car imaginatively named 'Miggy' (our family is rubbish at naming cars), the dreaded red box with a cross appeared where I wanted the DVLA to tell me the car's MOT had been renewed along with fresh tax. Then I'd be able to drive around in the hope I'd one day meet the owner in a Morrison's car park and stop for a chat, telling them, 'My dad used to own that car...'

I'd see that it was in good health, shake the person's hand and go home to complain, in private, about what was wrong with it, but comforted nonetheless in the knowledge that it was being looked after.

Foolishly, I decided to do some detective work.

I knew if the car was for sale it would be easy to find. Black wasn't a standard factory colour in 1976, so that narrows down a search for a black '76 Midget. The main problem seemed to be that Google wasn't having it that I wanted a Midget of that colour from that year, and was throwing up all sorts of answers to my request.

'Do you want a blue one? How about a yellow one? Does it have to be a '76? Look — a Mini!'

I thought it best to give up.

Then I saw him.

I was waiting outside Top Shop while my better half was in the process of trying stuff on, so I idly Googled the phrase 'MG Midget + 1796 + black + for sale' again. One came up, restored a few years ago, in lovely nick and at a price that was, annoyingly, slightly beyond my means. On the off chance it was Miggy I bookmarked the page and wrote down the number when I got home, where it stayed on my desk for a week.

So how do you react?

Of course, you give yourself another problem, after having put it off for a week.

I rang the Warwickshire-based garage where my dad's car was, not paying attention to the fact it was only 8.30am and they might not be in work yet, but I got an answer and asked for the man by the name I'd written down. A St Helens accent responded.

Ignoring what a man from the same town my dad's car once lived in was doing down in Rugby, I asked for the car's reg, my stomach churning with each of the first three letters as I finished the rest of it off for him.

My voice cracked as I asked the man if he would consider a part-exchange, a question he said he'd have to get back to me on after hearing the details and all about the (not great) condition of my own car — a sale I was already reluctantly considering.

'You're serious,' replied Sophie (that's my better half) when I texted her the news after informing Mum.

I'd already arranged a loan with my mother that would be paid back in very small instalments, to enable me to swap my car for the car which was formerly my dad's, and the garage had by this point called back to let me know there was a slight chance they'd meet me halfway on the cost front if they could take my Midget as a part-ex. I'd already made a mistake in putting my cards on the table. I wanted it.

Another option was to shift my car privately, but that would be a horrible experience as my car, for my own reasons, was sentimental to me.

I sat at the table to look at the pictures of Miggy again.

The car was in unquestionably good condition, undoubtedly more solid than my own car, which was a loud variety of orange called vermillion and a colour I'd wanted ever since I was a child. No one had changed the colour of NTB and even the luggage rack which was on when my dad had the car, was still there.

But there were problems, at least as far as I was concerned.

The non-original, but very cool fog lights my dad had on the front were gone and someone had put a wooden dash, steering wheel and gear lever knob in place. I hate wooden stuff where it's not supposed to be, so that would have to go.

There was also the need to question why I wanted the car. I know my dad was looking for it before he died and I needed to decide if I would be doing this for me or for him — and the car which was for sale is only really his in that it bears the same plate — almost everything else has been improved, fettled or changed.

Another point to consider was I already have one of my dad's cars, and when I asked Mum which one was more important to him, the answer was: 'The one he kept,' i.e, the one I had waiting in the garage for attention, which is a Magnette and not a Midget.

When push came to shove I just couldn't sell my car to finance this dose of nostalgia that wasn't really nostalgia because I wasn't around when my dad owned it. I actually got a lump in my throat when I thought about parting with my Orange Beast. It was my car with my story, despite its useless hood and cosmetic (I hoped) rust. It took a few days for me to let go of the idea of buying my dad's old car and letting someone else have their turn to enjoy it.

My mum also had a near-identical Midget I could drive whenever I wanted. But the car which really meant something to me was the one I'd not done enough about.

'Maggie' (that naming issue again) was all those things and more. When you look at the details in black and white, there could only be one decision really, and a decision I would be happy with, but not for a while.

'The one he kept,' was also a very important answer from my mother on another level.

There is, somewhere at my mum's, a photograph of the house I grew-up in just after it had been built. It would have been in the summer of 1985 and the houses in the picture have that certain new blankness that is only rubbed away once families move in, plant scrubs and paint walls. There is earth on all the front gardens where the grass is supposed to be.

None of this is significant — all new roads on new housing estates look like this when their owners haven't yet moved in. What is significant is that at the bottom of the drive of my parents' new house is a TVR 3000S. (KRE 893V — DVLA website says it's on a SORN, but as we've discussed, that doesn't necessarily mean bad news.)

At that time, my mum and dad only had my older brother, but you can imagine an MG Midget (by this point my dad's

Midget had been sold), a TVR and a 1950s MG saloon probably don't make up the most sensible stable of cars to drive around a new family. The TVR went.

I'm just grateful this happened about two-and-a-half years before I was born as I wouldn't have liked being the sole reason the car had to go. Sports cars out of a factory in Blackpool may not have been known for being easy to live with, but they still aren't something many would part with easily. On a side note, listening to and seeing a TVR burble past, you'd think it stands for something like Tyrannosaurus Velocity Rocket. It doesn't.

It stands for Trevor — an abbreviation of founder Trevor Wilkinson's name.

In my head, the selling of the TVR just before I was born was my parents moving out of the car phase of life and into the family one. The first 'everyday' car I remember was a red Ford Escort, and from a time before my memory started taking screenshots there was a Ford Fiesta XR2, which would be quite sought-after now. They're basically a chunkier, more powerful Fiesta.

An article written by my dad in January 1987 for *Enjoying MG*, which is the club magazine for the MG Owners' Club, confirms his passion for cars wasn't killed by having a family, though. Just because you're driving around in a modern car with a 'Baby on Board' sign doesn't strip you of any enthusiasm — as I was about to find out within a few weeks of writing this book, in early 2020, but that's another chapter within it.

The article appeared about a month before my parents found out I was on the way, and in it my dad explains that his love of cars came from a shopping trip to Southport in 1968.

It was here, the 13-year-old and an unwilling participant to the retail offerings of Lord Street, saw a nearly new 1967 MG BGT. Old English White, leather trim with black and red piping and a Les Leston wood rim steering wheel, he vowed, there and then, one day it would be his. (Les Leston was a British racing driver between 1956 and '57, starting only three races before becoming known for his motoring accessories business.) Personally, it isn't what I would have gone for. I'm not the biggest wire wheel fan and I don't like wooden steering wheels as a rule (and both are rules I sometimes break, like where Jaguar Mk IIs are concerned on the wire wheel front). That being said, when I was 13 I wanted to build a hot rod — tastes change.

My dad had already learned to drive by this point, in a borrowed 1935 Bentley 3½ litre on a borrowed field — sounds like a dream scenario for most youngsters, and in his article he lists six MGs owned since that fateful day in Southport. It's funny thinking that my own affiliation with the marque can be traced back to a single event in my dad's life.

He finally got the BGT. It was white, had wire wheels, and even the Les Leston, but it was a dud, as a lot of people undoubtedly found out in the '70s when they spent £350 on the car of their childhood dreams. This didn't put him off though, and he explains the purchase of Maggie was to save a friend's marriage, a Damask Red BGT was added to the collection because he liked Damask Red, and my mum's Midget was bought because it was black and two black Midgets would look good together.

There's a picture at the bottom of the article, and he's right — they do look good together — though the dream of having these five to choose from for the drive to work didn't last overly long as the TVR, BGT and one of the Midgets (my dad's) went before my brother was born in March 1985. My dad made reference to the XR2, calling it a 'hot hatch' which serves as a 'family hack', but said he thought it did the job well. It's worth noting though that at this point there was only James, my older brother, to ferry around and he wasn't quite two years old, so not in need of a great deal of leg room.

The car bug wasn't exclusively my dad's fault though. As you know, my mum has her MG, and before that she also owned a red Triumph Spitfire. It's just that my dad had an inability to just 'like' anything. If he was interested in something, he immersed himself in it, and anything with wheels were top of the list.

Interestingly, in the same mag in which my dad describes his car fever, an article about buying cars appears by a writer who went on to present a hugely popular car programme and then a well-known quiz show after he was removed from said car programme. I'm biased, but I think my dad's article is more entertaining than Jeremy Clarkson's and, while I certainly don't always agree with Clarkson, I do think he is a great writer. But if you knew my dad that opinion wouldn't be a surprise as he too had a knack of keeping a listener engaged while telling a story. My dad was also the secretary of the West Lancashire MG Owners' Club for a bit in the early '80s, and the newsletter editor, so his gift for writing had some outlet at least.

But journalism wasn't his calling, much to the benefit of the thousands of pupils he taught in St Helens from the late '70s until he died in 2014. He finished teaching pupils who, for a variety of reasons, couldn't be taught in mainstream schools, whether because of special educational needs or other circumstances that required a different setting. You can say with a lot of conviction that this made more of a difference to more lives than writing articles and books about cars.

Montego Man

Rover Montego
Top speed: 112 mph
0—60: 8.5 seconds
Economy: 35mpg
Cost when new: £6,159

There's an ever so slight problem with a classic car hobby when you have a family.

A lot of them only have two seats and the ones that have more than two sometimes don't have things like seatbelts, brakes which can pull-up a cantering vehicle at a moment's notice, or a reputation for withstanding impact. Many models also lack roof racks, boot space and legroom, so shopping trips and days out require more modern means of moving people around, and four-speed gearboxes which scream on motorways (added to the other issues mentioned) mean they are also not the most suitable choice for a day out.

Because of this, I would hazard a guess that many end up in the same position as my parents' MGs when families grow — in hibernation. It's not the case for all classic cars, granted. Some are loved, looked after and used, and at the other end of the scale many end up in the classifieds, but sentiment played a role once again in our house, and the MGs stayed pretty much untouched in the garage.

There was a risk of this pattern repeating as I prepared Maggie for her first outing in 36 years. The plan by summer 2020 was for me to have the car back from the specialist – who had done most of the work and put bits of the interior back together before the big day when we were back on the road – after having a safety check from a qualified mechanic. The issue was, I had hoped to be at this point a good handful of years ago and not when my wife was three weeks away from having our first baby. I was basically in the same position my dad was in when my older brother was preparing for his entrance into the world in 1985. I remain unconvinced that it's a coincidence my mum was pregnant the last time this car was road legal (sorry James, I *am* blaming you).

On a side note, you will more than likely be aware of why I was getting a 64-year-old car checked, but a quick explanation for those who aren't.

In the United Kingdom, a car made more than 40 years ago doesn't need to have an MOT, and vehicle tax on it is free, though you still need to go through the process of taxing it. You also need to shoulder the responsibility for keeping your car in a roadworthy condition, despite the absence of a need for an annual check. Even for custodians of cars which don't require a check, you can volunteer to have one, and there is a very compelling argument, on the grounds of safety, that you should have an MOT anyway. The last thing you want to do as an owner is overlook something and cause damage to anyone else (or yourself) so asking for an extra pair of eyes to have a look, especially on a car you know inside out and back to front, is probably a wise move.

Such technicalities were, of course, not a burden to me when I was of pre-school age and being ferried around in non-descript cars of the day which would now, quite rightly, take their place at certain classic car shows.

After the red Escort, there was the first real 'family' car, which was a light blue Montego estate.

Introduced in 1984, by the time we had a Montego it was the early '90s and these were, by this time, being built by the Rover Group and carried a Rover-shaped badge minus the longship and the word 'Rover'. These adorned the Montego until the last one was made in 1995. There was also a turbo version badged as an MG introduced in 1985, billed by the Austin Rover Group as 'the fastest production MG ever made' with a claimed top speed of 126mph. It cost £10,300 (a house was about £29,000).

We had two in the end — the Rover version, not the MG — and while my memories of the blue one are limited to just the colour, I have a much more vivid recollection of the maroon one which followed because of the seats in the boot. There's no other way to describe it — the hatchback opened to a normal-looking boot floor, and you could basically pull a bench seat up from being folded and chuck some kids in there, or a passenger you don't want to have to speak to.

I don't know if it was middle child syndrome or just because I was the most annoying of the three of us, but that bench in the boot was my domain, and I spent many, many miles travelling backwards as though on a train (but without an overpriced sandwich) while staring at whoever happened to be in the front of the car behind us.

It wasn't all bad on my own in the wayback seats. There was the odd occasion where a sibling would join me, but most of the time I had enough room on the bench to spread out comics and a notepad to write down numberplates I'd seen and occasionally a message for the driver behind, like 'help me' or, 'I can't see where they're taking me.' I got really told off for that one.

There were also side pockets for keeping things like old sweets in, which more often than not melted in the summer heat and welded themselves to the plastic. The only really rubbish thing about it were the times I'd have to share my space with shopping (I never worked out a strategy for delving into biscuits without my tampering with the packaging being noticed), although my parents would turn a blind eye to me helping myself to a 'No Frills' carton of orange juice on the journey home from the Kwik Save in St Helens. That brings back memories of the 'no such thing as a free carrier bag' — they were well ahead of the compulsory charge — and the occasions we'd go to Hanbury's, a chain of food shops in the North West bought by the Co-op in the 1990s. There, you would put your shopping in a cardboard box that had been used to deliver stuff to them, very forward thinking, but not great where space is concerned when you have a child in the boot. There was also the occasional cat when a trip to the vets was on the cards and they used to take what felt like forever, this being well before smartphones. Nor was reading by the glow of an orange streetlight in the back of that car the easiest way to pass the time.

At this point in life, however, my attention was also caught by something other than cars when a friend, Paul, introduced me to rugby league, at the age of seven, in 1994. The Magnette had already been off the road for a decade, but I was blissfully unaware as I allowed myself to be consumed by the sport completely for the next eight years, and off and on since.

It depends who you ask, but for a kid growing up near Wigan, it was a good time to be introduced to league and playing for Orrell St James (well, mostly standing on sidelines in a substitute's coat) developed into me amassing all there was to know about the game through newspapers, magazines and VHS tapes.

Playing rugby meant the Montego was pressed into Sunday-morning trips to muddy touchlines where it was always cold and nearly always wet. I use the word 'playing' rugby loosely as I spent nearly as much time on the touchline and watching the game as my dad. I'd wait to be called into action, unzipping the legs on my substitute's suit and wriggling them over my studded boots before trotting onto the pitch to replace a participant more favoured by the coaches, but on whom the magic sponge had not worked. But mostly my forays onto the pitch were just to enable me to lug two water bottle holders to team-mates.

This arrangement lasted longer than the Montego, which had suffered one or two breakdowns, including one because of a faulty fuel gauge resulting in an impromptu walk for chips, which I ate in the boot. That car also gave me — aside from dodgems — my first driving experience, when my dad sat me on his knee at the end of our road and let me hold the steering wheel while he very slowly, but also very illegally, put the car in motion. Even with the power steering I remember being overcome with anxiety that we were going to crash because I couldn't steer the thing, not for a moment thinking my dad would just press the brakes and bring us to a gentle halt — which he did.

A red 1995 BMW 518i followed, and when we first got that I had to get into a black bin liner after rugby before being allowed into the car. Eventually, though, we ran it into the ground and it got scrapped, but not before the lacquer went on the paintwork and made the bonnet fade to white.

Before its unceremonious end, my dad liked it so much he swapped the Fiesta he used for work (the BMW was my mum's) for a 318i, which was a bit older and had absolutely no leg room in the rear passenger seats.

All I remember about the Fiesta is that there were no seatbelts in the back. I once licked a spent cigarette end which was in the ashtray. My dad sold it with a cassette of 'Golden Brown' by The Stranglers still slotted into the car radio.

Around this time my grandparents had the aforementioned gold Escort, which permanently smelled of Go-Cat because my granddad kept some in the glovebox. He also kept some in the pockets of his corduroy trousers along with about a thousand pieces of kitchen roll, but in true eccentric-person style he could design, make and build literally anything.

As wonderful as it would be to own any of those cars now, they are unrelated to Maggie in that they were from a time in my life when the car was more something that I was aware of rather than something I loved.

But that was about to change.

The First Resurrection

MG Midget 1500
Top speed: 101 mph
0-60: 12.3 seconds
Economy: 26 mpg
Cost when new: £1,559

With two MGs in the garage, it was never going to take forever before they grabbed my attention.

It was the year 2000, I was 12. I recall the date with accuracy because it was during a few rugby seasons I spent at Haydock Warriors. Later that year, Wigan, the team I follow, lost the Super League Grand Final – a match to decide the champions of the competition – to St Helens. That was especially bitter for me because Haydock is a village which nestles in-between Wigan and St Helens and I was the only Wigan supporter in Haydock's team.

It was also around then that a stack of classic car magazines by the bathroom door caught my attention. I'm not entirely sure what such reading arrangements say about our family, and when my dad went into the garage for reasons such as retrieving tins of paint or the hosepipe, I would ask him about the cars instead of just giving them a passing glance.

Back then I knew nothing (and still know little) and in no way patriotic in my tastes by being drawn to British Leyland 'Friday cars,' whining gearboxes and bits that fall off. That nickname, for the uninitiated, was given to BL cars particularly overcome by Gremlins. The saying went that these cars were built on a Friday when the factory workers had their minds on other things, like the pub, rather than the job in hand.

I wanted a chopped Deuce Coupe like everyone else in history who had watched the film *American Graffiti* aged 12. A Chevy or a Thunderbird would do if I couldn't have the Coupe.

I'd always been drawn to social history, but flashing Coca Cola signs, rock 'n' roll and white T-shirts with squishy cig packets tucked into rolled-up sleeves are where my aspirations were at the time. My uncle lived in Boston (the one in Massachusetts, not Lincolnshire and, no, I never had chance to visit), so maybe that's where my Americanophilia came from. Joining my dad's stacks of *Practical Classics* and *Classic and Sports Car* on our bathroom floor were copies of *Custom Car* (as an advocate of print products I'm pleased to report all three are still going) before I really caught the bug.

Then something wonderful happened.

I can't remember why, maybe the financial burden of my parents having three children was beginning to level, but the Midget was brought out of hibernation. Whenever people asked my dad what gave him and my mum the shove to bring JED back to life, he said it was because it was sitting idle with a tank of fuel during fuel protest shortages. Obviously, that's rubbish, because the shortages didn't last for that long – and even if the car did have a tankful, it would have been beyond stale after x-number of years of being un-used. He was pulling everyone's legs.

Either way, the car didn't need much work to get it back on the road, just a fresh MOT. There were certainly no father/son moments in the garage where I would pass over tools and he'd show me how to fettle, but I was chief car polisher and that was a job I took very seriously. Never wash with water; polish on; clean cloth to buff off; do the chrome detailing carefully.

The results of my polishing were on show on the occasional school run, where a conversation between one of my classmates and dad would go:

'So that's really fast, then?'
'Not especially.'
'But it's dead rare...'
'Not really, no.'
'But it's smooth.'
'No.'

It's really easy to see why schoolchildren don't get it, and it's a point I will have to remember when my own are at the age where the Bugatti E-carbon Zer0, or whatever the must-have is at that time, speaks more to them than what will by then be a 70-odd-year-old gas guzzler (if you can still buy the stuff).

Back in 2000, it would have been a new Lotus 340R or Morgan Aero 8 that my classmates were comparing the Midget to; the concept of a classic car — and to many this is still the case — is to think enthusiasts like 'them old cars' because there must be some kind of enhancement, whether it be in value, performance, or driving experience. A lot of the time the only enhancement is enjoyment.

That was lost on me upon starting this book though because, nearly six years down the line (and a sum of money I roughly recollect but wish I didn't), I was yet to drive a car that was still in my garage. This was very much a case of hope, of twitching the curtains and frowning with envy when one of my neighbours took his own beloved vehicle out. When I drifted off to sleep each evening, I'd dream about going for a drive in ours.

Fast forward to 2020, and the big difference with the relatively easy coaxing of a Midget out of a decade or so of 'sleep' and the mammoth task of reviving Maggie comes down to time. It hasn't been kind to the Magnette. Thirty years off the road – when the project started – caused all sorts of problems from parts seizing-up to metal being lost with what seemed like every tick of the clock. I'm no welding specialist. Nor am I a specialist in fabricating panels and generally making many bits of rusty metal into one bit of not-as-rusty metal. In fact, I'm no specialist in anything car-related so there was no option but to find someone else who *could* halt time's cruelty. Before reaching that conclusion though, there were a few spurts of tinkering that ended in varying degrees of catastrophe, which we will get to. All of which means it was only in 2017, two-and-a-bit years after first getting the logbook for Maggie with my name on it, that proper restoration work began.

In the early days, most of it could be measured by phone calls which went a bit like this:

'Tom, it's about the car.'
(I know it's about the car because I know the number of the garage by heart now, and even then, it is saved in my phone.)
'Hi...' *Clears throat.*
'If you could come in and have a look, we can show you what we've been doing.'
'Ok, what have you done so far?'
'It's easier to show you. There are some decisions you'll need to make because I know you are mindful about cost.'

At this point the phone is already in my pocket and I'm heading for the door with the keys to my not very cool ten-year-old Vauxhall Insignia in hand, having dropped what I was doing at a second's notice. I've been known to leave paintbrushes in tins with a half-painted fence at the beck and call of the garage.

'Decisions need to be made,' means there are going to be bits of car where I don't want to see bits of car and holes on what is left of the car where I want to see the bits of car that are on the floor.

On arrival, I was more than once confronted with what looked like threequarters of a car, indeed in pieces on the floor, and two flimsy pieces of metal braced together on a ramp. I'm obviously exaggerating, but only a little bit.

It makes me realise how lucky we've been with our Midget — British Leyland's finest — or lucky in how our Midget was built on a Monday and not a Friday. But then again, were we unlucky? If the Midget hadn't been so easy to put back on the road, I might not have developed the same passion for old cars, and then, when my dad died, I might not have chosen such an expensive and emotionally draining grief project.

It wasn't as if the joy of a 60mph road in a diminutive open top early in life meant I was into cars and that was that, though. The road was far less straightforward. Teenage roadblocks such as music, being shy of the women in my peer group and then trying to impress them on the dancefloors of Wigan's finest social establishments, were also scenarios with which to contend.

Impossible to imagine now, but it seems there were once much more important things in life than spending time with your dad doing up an old car. It's utterly heartbreaking to think about, but that's what hindsight does to you. The same hindsight that says it might have been better to have admitted defeat a long time ago and buy someone else's dead dad's classic car which is in better condition than yours and will cost less money in the long run. But if we had the benefit of hindsight in the first place I think we'd end up in the wrong place and not as happy... eventually.

Or not as fulfilled, if happiness is the wrong word. As you're about to find out, if I'd had the benefit of hindsight I wouldn't have ended-up sitting here writing this with a baby due any day. I wouldn't have met their mum because I wouldn't have been at night school; I'd have done my degree years earlier. Hindsight would have robbed me of the chance to build the life I have now and, while I have struggles like many others, I would be very sad to think of a life without the people I have around me.

But before this gets mushy, because it's a car book, something happened before my growing love of internal combustion-engined transport got lost in a cloud of cigarette smoke on a dancefloor coated in a film of spilled Carlsberg.

My dad had me, for a few months, as his helper as I began to really pay attention to Maggie for the first time.

5

Maggie's First Attempt

2002 Vauxhall Zafira
Top speed: 117 mph
0—60: 12.1 seconds
Economy: 34 mpg
Cost when new: £12,850

A brisk clicking sound, like a cable tie being pulled tight, preceded the chuntering of an engine trying its best but not getting past turning over.

Those were the first sounds I had heard Maggie make and the excitement was high on a scale of nought to Christmas. I was 14. The clicking was the fuel pump, located in the boot, bursting into life and sending petrol from the tank to the engine, and the piercing cranking was made by my dad pressing on the starter button as the car rocked from side to side, like a sleepy, unfit bloke trying to run but only managing to stumble and cough.

Earlier that week, my dad had fitted a battery to the Magnette which he'd bought from Costco, and the very first sign of life I'd seen was the driver's side brake light, which was stuck on. I don't know why I was standing towards the back of the car, but that's what my memory is telling me was the first thing I saw, and dad's reaction to me telling him the light was stuck on tells me the size of the task, even then, was larger than he was expecting.

It was the summer holidays in 2002 and my little brother was about two months old, he'd been born seven weeks early and was the youngest by a fair stretch — 11 years behind my little sister — but having a new baby around the house didn't mean time spent with dad in the garage had to stop completely, even if our car-fettling sessions weren't as frequent as they might have been.

A new baby also meant our family's transport solution needed a capacity increase of one, so dad went with a Vauxhall Zafira. I'm sure he'd have thought his days of driving a seven-seater were up, but it did prove useful for my own needs a couple of years down the line.

I couldn't complain in the slightest though. Out of the four of us, I probably placed the biggest demands on my dad's time with cars and being taken to rugby training and matches. By that point I was playing rugby union for Orrell's junior section, which is seen by a proportion of the population in the North West as some kind of treason, and there are many books explaining more eloquently than I can why people feel that way even after more than 125 years of rugby being split into two separate sports.

Orrell was a once famous club which has since had to do a phoenix-rising as a result of some horrendous misfortune (I'm being kind to those responsible) not long after this part of my life, which also deserves a book in itself. They're now an amateur club and doing very well. My dad liked the rugby union club because there was a clubhouse which served coffee.

Anyway, back to the car and my parents' garage, which smelled of WD-40, stale petrol and a mixture of various open tins ranging from grease to paint, which make their own unmistakable hue. My grandad's garage was the same, other than as he was a carpenter, you can add sawdust to the concoction —

a wonderful and unique smell when it's all added together, which I fear is lost to me forever.

I was reminded of those few weeks with my dad when I came to replace the fuel pump on the first weekend of March, 2020. By this point, the word 'coronavirus' had made its way into every headline in every story we were reading, and we were days away from lockdown being brought in. That should have given me more time to play home mechanics, but the car was collected by the restoration company, which then had to close, meaning I spent lockdown with an empty garage.

Before those three months left me to get on with other things though, like completing a Masters and preparing for a baby's arrival, I had a cold afternoon free to bolt a new fuel pump where the old one had been.

Having already taken the old pump out, it was a simple case of fixing the new one onto the bracket and using the bolts I had sensibly put in an envelope with 'FUEL PUMP' scrawled on it and placed on a shelf in the garage next to a box of solar garden lights. Anyway, the screws on the bracket required a liberal dose of WD-40 to get them moving, and in doing so this caused the screwdriver to slip which led me to very nearly losing the finger that is home to my wedding ring. Okay, maybe holding the bracket in one hand and attacking it with a screwdriver held by the other wasn't the brightest thing I have ever done, but it still bloody stung when it slipped from the screw and into my flesh. Honestly, I'm not one for over-exaggerating!

With the bracket off, I then discovered the fuel line attached to the top still had some old petrol in it. And I did this by spilling it all over my new wound. At least the main objective of the exercise was complete by this point. Luckily, the nice new clean pump went onto the bracket without any problems, though I was very quickly reminded of the decapitating capabilities of the boot lid as I clambered in to fit it.

A few turns of a ratchet – held on each side of the bolts while in some challenging classic car yoga positions – did the job. I had thought about my dad every second of the job, because replacing the pump had been something on the list since shortly after those exciting few weeks in the garage in 2002. When we initially started with the Costco battery, the pump wasn't making that zippy clicking sound as soon as the ignition was turned on. At first there was nothing, and like anything that doesn't work when you call it into action for the first time in nearly 20 years, you hit it with a wooden mallet. That was my job, and one I was initially careful with (I was hitting a part of a classic car after all) until I was confident enough to give it my best shot each time my dad shouted, 'And again, T,' while listening for those telltale clicks. They eventually came and, of course, I assumed a working pump would mean I would be hearing the car run for the first time within minutes, rather than 18 years later.

Those clicks faded though, and while I can't remember exactly when dad and I stopped tinkering, I do know why.

6

Progress Stalled

1997 Ford Probe
Top speed: 132 mph
0—60: 10.6 seconds
Economy: 34 mpg
Legroom in the back: Nil.

It was the summer of 2003 and rock music, the thump of a bass guitar and wasting time dicking about with my fellow baggy-jeans-clad friends, had taken preference to summer afternoons in the garage with my dad.

Music had taken over everything else since a lesson in school the previous year, where a moment's boredom made me thrust my hand in the air when the teacher asked: 'Who wants to learn a bit of bass guitar?' It was one of the best moves I ever made.

Music lessons mainly consisted of sitting two to a keyboard and vamping chords over simple songs or 12-bar blues riffs, and that meant jostling for the best keyboards with bigger catalogues of pre-recorded demos on them and buggering about with the pitch and tempo of 'Hey Jude.' This particular lesson was playing along to Chris Montez's 1962 floor-filler, 'Let's Dance'. I use the word 'playing' loosely, and you can imagine the rattle of 30 kids tinkling the plastic ivories in unison with a *duh d—duh, duh* at the appropriate time.

You can also imagine what it must have sounded like when a lone electric bass joined the ensemble, but I felt unstoppable as I was shown the C, G and F notes required for our escapade. We were very fortunate to have a music teacher whose policy was to encourage instruments to be taken home from school for further exploration. And that was that. I was all about the bass.

There followed a period of six years when I was utterly convinced I was destined to be famous.

Every spare minute of time was devoured by playing music, although I was never great at guitar and fancied my piano teacher, so lessons in that were not a great success because I spent them in a trance.

I was, however, half decent on bass, and the only one of our small group of friends with the balls to sing, meaning I had to combine the jobs of singing and driving the bus in my first band — we were called Three Screws Loose. There were four of us.

It was very much a 'three chords and the job's a good 'un', with a guitar solo thrown in-type of arrangement, and victory at a school talent show helped us move from covering Green Day tunes to having a go at writing our own pop punk masterpieces.

At this point we were still in the midst of the Vauxhall Zafira years because baby brother was one-going-on-two. And while I was making use of the car's capacity for ferrying spotty friends and musical equipment across Wigan, Maggie was getting no closer to being out on the road.

I was much more concerned with mauling with guitar strings, allen keys and cans of electrical contact cleaner than venturing into the garage, though that would have been our next-door-neighbour's preference when it was my turn to host rehearsals.

There was one time when we had set up in my parents'

conservatory (admittedly not the most soundproof place to play ear-splitting pop punk) and we must have been three bars into the intro of our first song when I clocked the man in question through the front window. He wore a thick gold chain bracelet and smoked constantly. Sometimes we got on, but most of the time I was either making too much noise or squashing his flowers by (accidentally) kicking rugby balls over the fence.

'It's time, lads.'

We didn't practice at mine again after that, meaning my reliance on dad's driving and the Zafira were at least weekly. Instead of sitting in the boot among my own sticky sweets and old drink spillages, I was now in the very back of the three rows of seats behind little brother's attempts to follow down my path with his own food deposits in various car seat crevices, which can't be reached even with the most versatile Dyson attachment.

Our school talent show triumph prompted us to look into the wide world of gigging in public, swapping the smell of paper towels in school toilet changing rooms for the smell of stale cig smoke and spilled beer. The kind of social clubs which Peter Kay's *Phoenix Nights* was based on, and the kind of clubs you probably wouldn't want to leave your car outside, even if it was only a Zafira. My poor dad was mistaken for a taxi so many times while waiting for me and whichever bandmate was having a lift home.

At this stage in life, my bass-playing exploits weren't helping me in another area of life which 15-year-old boys become aware of, and things like idolising rugby players, *Pokemon* card collections, computer games and messing about with cars in the garage with dad get cast aside as a result. Women.

I'd gone from the round short kid in class with no hope in the world of catching anyone's eye, to being the skinny, spotty, short kid with long hair with no hope of catching anyone's eye.

Until I did.

Girls came with warnings. From dad, from my mum, from my guitar teacher.

'You can either be famous, or have a relationship, not both,' my guitar teacher said, putting a fag out in the ashtray balanced on top of his amp.

We were in my guitar teacher's flat in St Helens. It had no carpet, but oddly a can of carpet glue on the windowsill, and was littered with musical equipment in varying stages of decay. He was showing me some blues riffs (they're riffs on bass, licks on guitar, he would say) and seemed genuinely concerned.

The girl in question was the year above me, but at a school in St Helens, and we met on the 352 bus while I was on my way home from a Saturday not doing very much in Wigan town centre, the chosen location for teenagers of a certain cultural persuasion that summer. The bus was probably a DAF SB120 for anyone who's interested, but can't be 1,000 per cent sure about it.

With the warning from my guitar teacher came a warning from my mum too. She was being protective, I think, but cited worries about schoolwork and the time I would now not be spending playing bass.

Dad: 'What does her dad drive?'

The answer was Ford's replacement for the Capri.

Well, it's really a Mazda, in that it is the result of Ford's collaboration with Mazda and apart from the blue oval badge on the front it looks just like a Mazda. These days it enjoys a cult following, possibly because of the name, which lends itself to endless innuendo. Or possibly because it *is* a bad car. Or possibly because some people genuinely do like them and don't think they are bad cars at all.

People cite reasons such as poor build quality like big panel gaps, or a harsh ride, or the fact that even at a reduced price of £12,700 in 1994 it was expensive.

The type of bad car behaviour which gains cult status is the kind of thing I'd fall in love with these days, but in the summers of 2003 and 2004 my main problem with the Probe was that there was no room in the back whatsoever. This made lifts home very uncomfortable. Her dad's problem with the Probe was that the petrol light was always on. This was an especially big problem when his daughter and her new acquaintance wanted lifts home. To those unfamiliar with how the land lies between the rival towns of Wigan and St Helens, the no-man's land in the middle is a hilly little village called Billinge.

Going off topic slightly, but so you can picture the setting of this story, Billinge is divided into two ends — Chapel End, where the Anglican St Aidan's Church is and further down the hill is St Mary's Catholic Church. And then there's Higher End, which is basically higher up the hill.

Chapel End is in St Helens, and Higher End is in Wigan — roughly speaking.

Between my parents' house in Higher End and where she lived in St Helens, the other side of St Helens, is a regular affordable bus service, which would have been the sensible solution to the Probe's thirst for petrol. I wouldn't be surprised to hear if it cost her poor dad in excess of a fiver a trip.

The issue we had was that the last bus for the first leg of my journey home, from hers to St Helens, was at 20 past nine in the evening, and when you take getting home from school, getting changed and getting a bus between the two, four hours twice a week just wasn't enough time for us to do nothing together except not do homework, play bass or see our friends. No, an extra 40 minutes was essential, meaning we were either taxied from Billinge to St Helens like royals in my parents' Zafira, or taxied from St Helens to Billinge like squashed-up royals in her dad's Probe.

For someone with a Probe, it was entirely appropriate for her dad also to have a Capri.

You'll know that a Ford Capri calls to a certain type of car enthusiast and you can see exactly why someone with a Capri would also use a Probe as their daily. They have an image which veers towards brown leather jackets, stale cigarette smoke and greasy hair, though you could argue the 1970s luvverman man image is more than a little unfair, and is certainly unfair on this particular Probe owner, who was never anything but nice to me.

These days Capris aren't cheap. Like anything that had a whiff of a '70s image, which was uncool and 'past it' in the early noughties, the stuff which survived the next 20 years has been reborn as retro cool. You can part with money well north of £20,000 for the right Capri, which seems like an awful lot to live out a fantasy where the owner is Bodie from *The Professionals*, but then others will have their own views on my own car predicament.

Back in the early noughties Capris hadn't quite reached their status as a car people flock around at car shows, and it — to my mind at least — still had the whiff of Brut masking cigarette smoke. But her dad's car was a long way off having its plaid fishnet interior graced by a thuggish agent who stomps his right foot to the floor, producing a comical sound from a smokey wheelspin before thrashing off into the St Helens traffic only to be stopped at a red light 100 yards later.

That's because this particular Capri had no wheels and rested in the front yard under a tarpaulin.

Across the country there are many cars like this in yards, sometimes covered, sometimes up on bricks, always rusty and nearly always 'too far gone.' In such scenarios the owner almost never admits defeat by selling their car to someone else looking for a project, and when they do that person is almost always as well-intentioned and equally doomed to failure.

I can't honestly say what the outcome was for this particular Capri. Whenever I went round on a Saturday he was, most of the time, underneath it, patch welding the bits that were either corroded or falling off, which could have been most of it, I don't know.

Looking back it would have been an opportune time to learn something. Sure, there are better quality restorations than what most can achieve while lying on flattened crisp boxes on damp and uneven flagstones, but some lessons in how to at least use the welding kit could have gone a long way to one 16-year-old's future aspirations.

Instead, I had other things on my mind, like hanging around McDonald's on the St Helens linkway and not getting the bus home.

7

My Own Wheels

2002 Vauxhall Agila
If you ask a four-year-old to draw a car it will look like a 2002 Vauxhall Agila. Another case of badge engineering, it is actually a Suzuki Wagon R wearing a Vauxhall badge. To learn in, it was a difficult car to drive. To be seen in it was even more difficult.

Imagine an egg box with little button wheels pinned to it. I'll concede that the KAs, Puntos and Yarises that my friends drove around in weren't exactly a passport to the top table on the social scale of the college I went to, but I'd have swapped in a heartbeat.

Not even just with the really lucky ones who had a Vauxhall Corsa. I'd even have had a beaten-up Fiesta in the corner of the car park, though I would have taken off the beaded seat cover.

What I was driving in was the social equivalent of refusing to wear deodorant.

To the uninitiated, the Vauxhall Agila is basically a box with tiny wheels, which look comically small for the vehicle they are supporting.

Not quite Reliant Robin unstable (an unfair assumption in my book, but another discussion for another day) the Agila's height does make it look like it may topple over if a corner is taken a little too enthusiastically. With an awkward driving position, tiny pedals and a gear lever you have to stretch to reach, it was a difficult car to learn to drive in.

My dad used the Agila for work. The idea was that he would have a cheaper car so I could learn alongside my older brother without there being too much worry about what sort of effect two clumsy teenagers would have on the more delicate parts essential to the vehicle's functioning. Crunching gears and stalling on empty car parks is not something he would have wanted either of us to do when he had the BMW.

Three Screws Loose had, by this point, played its last sticky-carpeted pub and I was in a new band with new ideas. The fun pop punk had been replaced by angsty indie and my shoulder-length hair was more akin to the mop you often find on top of someone shrouded in a trench coat. I'd met the members of the new band in college and they were from Leigh. That meant asking them for lifts, and then needing lifts home from either parents or band members. Sometimes it meant getting a bus from Leigh to Billinge, via Wigan, with bass equipment in tow. It wasn't working out and it didn't last long.

I think the fact I developed a bad clutch-riding habit early on, and nearly took out a police car when making a right turn on a country road during an early outing with dad didn't help my case when asking for more practice, and my progress was almost as slow as the non-existent progress being made on Maggie.

This meant that as far as getting to gigs and rehearsals went, I still needed taxiing in the Zafira — which was more of a problem now because of yet another new band situation.

The spring and summer of 2006 felt like the time I was thrown around Silverstone in an Aston Martin by a professional driver. It 'only' reached 147mph but it started to snow halfway round and the back end fishtailed once. This experience was like that but for six months instead of 60 seconds.

I was making a very good job of ballsing-up my A Levels and there were four reasons for that, but one of them, looking back, was really quite pathetic.

The girl whose dad had the Capri on blocks had come to her senses the year before, and my response was to play Damien Rice's *O* album on repeat and pretend I liked red wine — which I now do but, like beetroot, it was something I grew into. Anyway, this false moping and modelling myself on a singer-songwriter/ Bernard Black from *Black Books* crossover didn't do my image or my AS levels any good. What it did do, when combined with reasons two and three, which were the smoking shelter at college and The Station pub a few hundred yards away (now flats, RIP), was help me on my way to returning D grades in my exams with the exception of English, for which I scraped a B. I went to a college where grades like this didn't happen, spending so much time wallowing over an acoustic guitar in need of restringing and a better player that I took my eye off how, if I got my head down and did some work, the next ten years would've been a lot easier.

Then came reason four.

Joining a rock band called The Gekko made me absolutely, 100 per cent sure I was going to be famous. It sounds ridiculous because every 18-year-old who has ever been in a band thinks that, but we really had a reason to believe that summer that my exam results really wouldn't matter at all.

Why? Two words.

Bon Jovi.

In the June, four months after joining the band, I was on stage in front of tens of thousands of people as the support act for one of the biggest bands in the world.

To cut a medium-sized story short, Bon Jovi used their tour that year to help local bands by offering support slots as prizes. For Manchester, the radio station Key 103 ran the competition, and from the demos sent in, three were picked for a battle of the bands style final in Manchester — at two days' notice.

I was at work when I took the call — I sold mobile phones and would have either got the bus or a lift from dad into work — and immediately left the shop floor to ring our drummer.

'We're rehearsing tonight, mate,' I said. It took him and the other three no convincing whatsoever that their plans for the evening would not have been better than rehearsing when I told them the details of the call I'd just taken.

For me, as well as cancelling plans (I didn't have any) the news meant arranging lifts, both to rehearsal and into Manchester on a weeknight to play a gig. Luckily, as well as having a very supportive father, there was some personal pride in it for him as he had helped enter us into the competition.

Dawson's music shop had a branch in St Helens at the time (I bought a Fender Strat from them with the money I'd saved icing gingerbread men at Sainsbury's and got good at drawing various parts of the anatomy with a piping bag, but I never had the nerve to hide those in packs for sale). Anyway, to enter the competition, you could either take a demo CD into Dawson's or email Key 103 an MP3. We did both. As my dad worked in St Helens, he took the demo into Dawson's for us, and no doubt told everyone within earshot how brilliant his son's band were. He was convinced we were going to win, even before a shortlist was drawn-up. To be honest, so was I. It wasn't big-headedness. Well, maybe it was, but it's hard to describe. I was riding on the crest of the biggest, smoothest wave of my life.

I just couldn't bloody drive.

My lift to rehearsal that evening was in our drummer's Citroën Saxo. It was blue and had one of those CD players where the front clips off so that the radio doesn't get stolen while you're in Asda, though I can't remember the last time I ever read about a car radio being stolen. If you'd have seen everyone's car radios when we were kids you'd think it happened all the time. Both my parents' BMWs had removable radios, but they were really big, handbag-sized, and quite heavy, so anyone breaking into the car will have known to look under the front passenger seat for the radio (where it always was), because there's no way anyone would carry it around with them. After a while the connections became unreliable because they were worn out with all the pushing in and pulling out of the radio, meaning it didn't work properly anyway. My enduring memory of my dad's 318i was our Sunday morning drives to whichever freezing cold village on the Pennines was hosting the junior rugby match that required my dad to stand on the touchline. He'd let me play whichever mix tape I'd made to get me in the right frame of mind for the game, and sometimes it worked. More often than not, though, I was a substitute and therefore standing with him to watch the game, so by the time I got on in the second half was invariably freezing too. Any psychological benefits provided by Green Day with the volume turned up to 11 were long gone.

The Citroën's CD player suffered from a similar affliction — to get it to read discs you sometimes had to punch it.

On the night of this rehearsal, though, no punching of CD players was needed as our drummer picked me up from my parents' house and loaded the car with my equipment (and any drummer and bass player lift-sharing combos will appreciate the Tetris-like satisfaction of loading a small car with an entire drum kit, bass and amp — I'm sure we aren't the only ones). We travelled in silence to rehearsal.

After that rehearsal, my next car journey was to a bar in Manchester city centre for the battle of the bands-style grand finale to see who would get to support Bon Jovi and it was in my dad's Zafira. There were two other bands on the bill, and considering the gig was arranged at just a few days' notice, and it was a mid-week show, the queue of people outside the venue resembled the wait to be let into Asda in the first Covid lockdown, just closer together.

We obviously arrived early, sound checked and were given a run through of what was going to happen with the general running order. We were subject to the usual: 'You can't park here,' from six-foot-four security men before the explanation that you're an *artiste* and they wave you through into the loading area like they're responsible for getting precious cargo onto a plane.

All I had to load in was a pathetically small bass amp and my trusty Fender Jazz — there was even room in the car for my little brother, now aged four, to come along for the ride. Dad, ever supportive, was going to take him home before coming back to cheer us on. In the venue there was a run through from a man from Key 103.

'The bands will all play their slots and then The Gekko, sorry, the winning band will come back on to play an encore.'

We could feel the daggers from the other bands like they were really blades being poked into our eyes. Had the judges already decided?

That doesn't matter. What does matter is that about a month later, when Bon Jovi were taking a limo from their dressing room at Manchester City's ground to the stage — at the other end of said ground their support's bassist was waiting outside the gates in the back seat of his dad's Vauxhall Zafira trying to ring the number of the person at Key 103 he'd been given so that the security personnel would kindly let his band in.

It was a much less embarrassing situation than it might have been had I been able to drive and taken the Agila to my date with rock n' roll destiny.

I say destiny, but what actually happened was after we had played our set, we were allowed to watch some of Bon Jovi's performance before being told to get our equipment shifted from the empty executive box we were in (complete with empty fridge) and being booted out of the stadium to a glorious June sunset while the headliners' encore was in progress. Some people were leaving, maybe to beat the traffic, and a family stopped us and insisted we sign their programmes. Programmes must have cost upwards of a tenner — even back in 2006 — and I still feel bad for defacing theirs but they insisted. My lift home was in the Saxo with our drummer — I can only imagine what Richie Sambora and Co went home in.

For me, there were a few more months of cadging Saxo lifts. Rehearsals, gigs and recording sessions that were highlighted by punching CD players, smoking and games of band equipment Tetris. Then the day of my driving test came in the early autumn.

I learned to drive in a Ford Fiesta — that was the instructor's car — and when I wasn't with him I was nearly taking out police cars with my dad in the Agila. He's the only passenger I've ever had who has used the handle on the ceiling, though he was also using his other hand to flick cigarette ash out of the window as he used the end of one cig to light the other. I definitely didn't do his blood pressure any good.

Anyway, the day of the test came and I knew I had failed when I turned left onto what I thought was a one way road that wasn't, and was far over to the right when pulling onto to the next street.

'We're on the wrong side of the road now, so be extremely careful,' was the examiner's less than helpful words as I pulled out.

It was one of two major errors — I hadn't even noticed I'd failed to stop at a 'give way', and much to my disappointment I didn't emulate dad by passing first time. He actually passed on his 17th birthday, helped by learning to drive in that field, aged 12.

I honestly can't remember what happened in between, other than I know I rehearsed with the bad which meant I either got a lift in a Saxo or a Zafira and I must have bussed it to the shop to peddle mobile phones to fund my weekends on £1.50 bottles of Carlsberg while bopping to emerging bands and trying to impress girls from college with my new-found Jovi fame.

No one would have wanted anything to do with my wheels, even if anyone did look at the bass player in a punk rock band with vibes of My Chemical Romance-meets-Green Day. At the time, the fashion was trench coats and mop haircuts, which I didn't get the memo for, and it's important to add that my lack of success was in no way down to fashion choices or having a crap car.

I was more fortunate in my second driving test, having collected more minor faults than I was ok with admitting, but luckily no majors. It certainly wasn't pretty, and my 'thank fuck for that' didn't go down too well with the examiner when she told me I'd passed, quickly pointing out that I needed to pay more heed to where the kerb was when I was asked to pull into spaces — but it didn't matter.

What did matter was that I could now go where I pleased — petrol money permitting — and the fact my wheels were the most unfashionable in town didn't matter.

I had recently decided university wasn't going to be for me — Damien Rice-influenced A level results in hand — and decided I was going to see if this band would make it. And I didn't need fancy wheels anyway because I was in a new relationship and lived for Friday nights on the pop. I got to where I needed to be and how I did it wasn't important — bus, Agila, lifts, I didn't care.

And at that point in my life I couldn't have cared less about a 50-year-old MG saloon still sleeping in my parents' garage. I was riding high and quickly moved out of my parents' home and into a flat in town, with a job selling tools (I didn't know the first thing about grades of sandpaper or screwdriver heads, but who cared — I was going to be famous) and certainly didn't care about cars or pretending to like cars to impress my dad.

It must have killed him, but my mind was made up. I was turning off at this point and taking my life into the unknown.

The main thing I learned, vehicle-wise, was that you can fit a surprising amount of cheap flat-packed furniture from Ikea into an Agila if you fold the seats down.

8

Driving Up the Wall

Citroën Saxo
A Saxo was driven by everyone from chavs to the Gavins — lads who liked football and hair gel but not really cars, but they still didn't want a really crap one. It wasn't driven by rock drummers. Except ours. It's not a large car, but you can fit a bass guitar, cab and full drum kit in the back with the seats down.

This account of a life is based around cars — and one car in particular — but for a long time cars just didn't feature in this life at all. When I moved out — and into the flat above a shop in Wigan, almost exactly like in the Pulp song — the Agila didn't come with. I could walk to work, get lifts to rehearsals and gigs.

I lived in town and didn't need to drive. So didn't.

It's very hard to look back now and try to pick holes in what I did versus what I 'should' have done when I turned 18.

If I'm being perfectly honest, if I could have had my time again, I would have stayed at home, gone to university to read English, had a few pints of a Friday evening and come home to learn classic car maintenance from a local garage while helping my dad on Maggie.

I can't have my time again though and what happened was nothing, unless you count the decay of my relationship with my dad. Maybe that's unfair, as I also believe you are the sum of your experiences, another dad lesson — hey! Every day's a school day — but we're using the Magnette as a metaphor and that wasn't getting any better at this point so let's go with it.

I would occasionally borrow the Agila, for things like camping trips and furniture shopping escapades, but in reality my driving became less frequent. Rehearsals were covered by our drummer's blue Saxo, as were gigs, probably to his annoyance but he very rarely, if ever, complained.

My own driving became so infrequent that I became a very nervous driver and would actively avoid driving even if borrowing the Agila was possible, but our drummer and I had a lot of fun in the Saxo, punching the CD player, fitting a full drum kit and bass rig into the back and filling the floorspace with rubbish.

I wasn't even interested in cars, not even the MGs at my parents' — they were a distant memory and I wasn't the least bit bothered about any future resurrection of either car, and this went on for years.

My exodus from the semi-rural Billinge to the great metropolis that is Wigan showed no signs of changing, and when I bought a house (without a garage) any future classic car escapades looked scrapped before they had started.

The closest I got to getting any form of joy from cars was a trip to the 2009 British Grand Prix at Silverstone. The singer in our band knew how to get us onto a stewarding rota, which saw us paid £60 or so a day for keeping an eye on the crowd, and in return, we got to stand and watch the race weekend from stands people had paid hundreds to sit in. I have to admit, it was an easy gig — people who can afford to sit at the Grand Prix don't tend to be too rowdy.

Disappointingly, championship leader Jenson Button finished sixth, with world champion Lewis Hamilton all the way back in 19th. Still, some sort of classic car joy in me was rekindled with how much I enjoyed the vintage racing at the end, though judging by the number of people left of the 128,000 crowd I was in the minority. For my troubles, I also got sunburnt, and spent most of what I was paid on beer, cigarettes (which wasn't my fault, as I was an idiot and back then they were still branded and came in a novelty metal tin, and sold by women with not very many clothes on) and a McLaren cap.

Along with our singer, the drummer joined us, of course, and the Saxo was our carrier.

Crucially, that joy from vintage racing opened up a very narrow door with my dad, who still undoubtedly harboured hopes of me wanting to get stuck in on the MG with him one day.

We went on a marshalling taster day at Oulton Park. Dad picked me up and we spent the day together, just like when he used to drive me around to rugby matches when I was a kid.

Dad hoped this would spark a renewal of us spending time together and was pretty serious about us doing the course and then becoming fully-fledged marshalls together, but I was less than receptive to his olive branch, and looking back I regret this now as it would have been a lot of fun.

Around this time I stopped seeing eye-to-eye with a lot of important people in my life. Dad and I fell out once or twice over trivial things, while my reluctance to drive anywhere was partly to blame for friction in the band.

You've probably guessed that by this point that we were not famous. I was an admin assistant for the local council after initially processing orders for the tool shop when I first moved into town, and fame seemed further away with each half-empty pub we played in the aftermath of the Bon Jovi high.

The problem wasn't that our drummer was unwilling to give

me lifts, his attitude was: 'I'm going anyway,' but one particular fly in the ointment was the size of bass rig you can fit in a Citroën Saxo along with a full drum kit meant we would often have to ask to borrow the rig from another band on the bill — or hope there was a house amp. Bands don't like sharing equipment, and house amps aren't always the most well looked-after pieces of equipment.

I can remember the exact moment I knew my band was going to go down the toilet, but it was a long time before it actually happened. After the Jovi gig, a man from a big record label got in touch to say they liked our sound, and wanted to meet-up to have a chat about taking us on as a project band — it would have meant devoting everything time-wise to the band and for the paltry sum of £30 a week. We met in a pub near Horwich, not far from where Bolton Wanderers play, and again I got a lift in the Saxo. Delicately sipping a Diet Coke (my disposable income was around £20 per week, making pints a luxury) I informed the man that the record we were working on at the time was slightly different in how it sounded to the pop punk anthems he had listened to and said he liked. I looked nervously across at my bandmates.

'You've changed your sound?'

The enquiry struck me in the chest — I knew at this point, because of how he had said it, that he wasn't interested anymore.

'It's more that it has developed naturally than it has changed,' our guitarist helpfully explained.

In truth, what had actually happened is our sound *had* changed — almost beyond recognition — and the record we were working on simply wasn't as strong as what was already out there, if more serious. Still, we managed to convince our man that visiting us in the studio we were recording in was a good idea. He agreed, and a few weeks later the nail in our hope's coffin was firmly hammered in as we sat in the small studio in a house near Blackburn. It was a cold night and everyone was tired — a kind of tiredness unique to the end of a few days' recording — and he looked up from his hands which were cradling a cracked mug of tea and started to comment on a track he thought had finished which hadn't. When it kicked back in he went quiet, as did our chances of his label picking us up.

The band battled on through gigs in stinky empty pubs and gigs in crammed stinky pubs. There were some great songs and some not so great, and there were discussions and exacerbations and good nights and silent drives home after bad ones.

To make transportation matters worse, the Saxo had been swapped for a Micra while the drummer returned to university and our ability (or willingness on my part) to transport bass equipment was further compromised. I had also started to try to make inroads into journalism at this point, and the final straw for me was when I was regularly opting to take a laptop in a shoulder bag, via public transport, to freezing cold press boxes to type out match reports for free than drive, or be driven, to play songs I wasn't overly into for free.

I would like to point-out that listening back to the songs in the band's later years now, I am not offended by them at all. I actually quite like them. But I still had much more fun playing happy poppy rock than the metal with the screams and the roars. I wanted something more in the middle when we were getting more 'grown-up' in our sound, but my fear of conflict prevented me from speaking up, and resulted in sadness. This led to me not trying anymore. Yep, it was my fault. The band split-up and I needed lifts no more.

It seems strange that the shortest chapter in my affiliation with Maggie covers such a long stretch — almost six years — but something was about to happen which would give me back that bond with the road.

9

Starting Over

2005 Vauxhall Corsa SXi
More associated with those people who knacker tyres and clutches at night on industrial estates, this was a left-field choice when my mum bought hers new. Whatever I thought of it, I will be forever grateful for this car giving me back my freedom.

Five years and seven months after I left sleepy Billinge for the bright lights of Wigan I came home.

I can very clearly remember calling my mum (always the first person you ring, isn't she?) and asking her, very calmly, to pick me up. It was a Friday morning and I'd pre-warned my boss at work the day before that I would probably not make it in because of what I knew was about to happen on the Thursday evening. We'll leave the details and the whys, but the initial calm nature of my reaction descended into me being quite bitter and angry, and this lasted for a good few months, during which time my reaction to the situation wasn't very gentlemanly and I said things I am not proud of. I have since apologised but it doesn't make it ok. It was the morning of Friday, 13th April, 2012. Do I leave it, as I have done for a long time, or do I make contact and properly apologise for my part in the aftermath? I'll probably never know, but we've since spoken in a civil manner and everyone has moved on.

Anyway, back to the scene. Mum collected me in her car as my dad was working, and I remember how upset she was on the drive home that things hadn't worked out. On that first day I felt okay. I had a pub lunch with my sister and started to think about the financial freedom I would have to go to university if I moved back home (something I didn't do when I left college — I was going to be famous, remember).

I had a problem with going home though, and because the drummer (and my taxi driver) from the band was still good friends with me — by this point he was also engaged to my sister — his parents agreed I could move into their spare room on a temporary basis. I could walk to the nearest train station for work, and could start to think about my options. I hated my clerical job, to be honest I didn't have much of a clue what I was doing for most of it, and the more I wormed my way into press boxes at rugby league matches to write poorly-written reports for what was by this point poor pay packets, the more I knew I had to qualify as a journalist, though when I found out what qualifications I needed, I chose to do it on a part-time basis so I could still turn up to work and enjoy some form of financial comfort.

But first, my dad had another job for me.

He picked me up one Saturday morning in my mum's car — a seven-year-old Vauxhall Corsa which she had just replaced with a Mini, not a proper one, sadly.

Dad drove to Skelmersdale and pulled over on a quiet road.

'Right, swap over.'

I was 17 again. Nervous, my hands were shaking as I tried to adjust the mirrors and work out where everything was. The occasional rattle of a car flying past didn't help and the smell of my dad's cigarette was making me want one — though I'd never dare ask.

The car was in a different universe to the Agila. The steering wheel was trimmed in leather and felt sporty, the gear lever felt robust and was in a much better place, the driving position was lower down. I liked it.

The only difference between this and my few drives with dad in the Agila was that this time I was supposed to know what I was doing. I had, after all, passed my test on my second attempt almost six years before, but my confidence was shot, more than likely due to the years I'd spent in the passenger seat. There was that shaking again, my foot wouldn't behave as the wobble went up my leg as I pressed the pedal to the floor, my dad's calm voice telling me to indicate and check before moving — and I'm sure at the time I was cursing him under my breath for being patronising.

But in truth I was a little bit scared, and like having someone reading over your shoulder, driving someone else can make you do things you wouldn't normally. You become really aware of every movement all of a sudden.

'You're dipping me into the kerb a bit here, mate.'

'Ok, ok, just please stop putting pressure on me.'

I wasn't that polite.

I was dipping the clutch and coasting, my road position was woeful and I was getting annoyed with my dad's coughing — well, the fact he would have a coughing fit and then spark up again. But he was doing me a huge favour so I put up and shut up.

A 2005 Vauxhall Corsa, especially in 2012, was basically a chav mobile. It was boy racery for the people who couldn't afford a souped-up Focus and most other Corsas driven by people my age had one too many of their mates in the back seat and smelled of a different inhalationary product to the one currently stinking out this one.

But it was the best car I had driven at that point in my life. Come to think of it, for what it was, it is still up there. I don't know if that says more about me or the car.

Corsas have felt very plastic-y by comparison since. We had one as a pool car at the newspaper I worked at in the mid-2010s — I realise this is a while ago now — and they lacked oomph and felt more like a car for a retired person for taking to Asda than a Burberry cap-wearing wannabe public menace.

But I quickly gained my confidence and learned to love what became mine. My parents just gave it to me — fantastic.

Despite being 24 and having held a licence for five and a bit years by that point, I was essentially a new driver on the road and trips across the M62 to try and launch my journalism career at rugby league grounds scattered across The Pennines could be described as varying degrees of hairy.

There was a journey to a rugby union ground in Bradford to cover a rugby league charity day and my sat nav insisted the venue was a gate to a field, which was void of rugby posts but full of sheep. Then there was the drive back from Hull in the rain when I didn't respect the conditions and was lucky not to aquaplane as I flew into the outside lane in next to zero visibility with the house in the middle of the motorway to my right.

As a side note, and this *is* loosely driving related, if you've ever driven through West Yorkshire on the M62, you will have seen Stott Hall Farm in the middle of the motorway and you will have wondered why the bloody hell it's there. If you haven't seen it, just jump onto any social media platform and search for 'M62 House' and you'll find it easily.

There is a story which I wish wasn't a myth, that the farm is still there, with its little tunnel under the westbound carriageway for access, because the farmer refused to sell-up when the bulldozers came along to start building the motorway in the 1960s.

It's a story which is certainly believable — not to stereotype farmers from West Yorkshire, but I'm sure a West Yorkshire farmer wouldn't mind anyone saying they'd be stubborn enough to tell the builders of the M62 that they can build around him because he isn't selling up.

The truth is less romantic though. The house is still there because of the way the land lies, there's a geological fault beneath the house and it would have been much harder to knock the house down and level the land off for a road instead of just going around it, and this makes sense to anyone who has driven it and noticed that westbound is considerably higher than the eastbound side — and if you're fortunate enough not to be concentrating on the road because you're a passenger, the view is beautiful. The dramatic scenery of the moors is really quite haunting — more so in winter when it's going dark at 3.00pm and sheets of Biblical rain add to the drama.

Further to the west, on those drives home from covering matches in Yorkshire, is the highest point on the M62, and the highest point on any UK motorway at 1,220ft above sea level. It's near the Pennine Way footbridge at the border between Yorkshire and Lancashire and you know you're there because there's a big blue sign that states the fact as you approach junction 22 at Rishworth Moor.

It's a really interesting part of the motorway — you've got the Windy Hill transmitter to your left if you're travelling westward, and the footbridge, 65ft above the carriageway, was built to accommodate walkers on the Pennine Way route which opened in 1965. I've never walked it but, apparently, if you have a good coat and the stomach for bitter winds which you can lean into, it's beautiful.

When I was younger and more immature I used to boo as I drove past the white rose milestone when going into Yorkshire, and cheer on the way home going in the opposite direction, but whichever side you are on, you can't not be amazed at the atmosphere up there — yet thousands of people thunder along that route every day — except for a Friday night when the thundering becomes a slow crawl.

I don't think I've ever been as tired when driving as I have on that motorway when coming back from a match at Headingley in Leeds, or Hull. Being part of the press, we drove home long after the supporters had come off the motorway and meandered back into Wigan, with scarves flapping from back windows. There's a feeling of freedom and loneliness wrapped into one when you're driving along a quiet motorway on your own. I used to open the window a crack to help me keep my concentration, feeling the biting cold against my ears as the wind whipped in and kept me company. The irony is that as tired as I was when pulling onto the drive at my drummer's parents' house, I was never able to sleep once I'd got inside.

It was a good summer, 2012, looking back, though I spent a lot of it in traffic and in a poor state of mind given the fallout of my relationship. One thing about moving out of Wigan was the drive into Wigan for work. It was horrendous. Wigan to Orrell is a three-and-a-half-mile drive, which could take 45 minutes at 5.00pm, and more than once I considered walking as that would only take about 20 minutes longer — though at least while sitting in traffic you have some cover if it starts to rain.

But driving didn't play any role in the biggest change in my life up to that point, though the change, in a way, brought about my reacquaintance with cars.

It involved trains. Mostly the Pacers that the rail company Northern only retired in 2020, despite them being well past their 20-year lifespan.

Pacers are brilliant. They stink of hot oil, are very noisy and uncomfortable. They were built between 1980 and 1987 and were supposed to be a stop-gap even then. When a Pacer leaves a station, it sounds like a tractor pull at a country show and smells like the drains of a backstreet garage which does dodgy MOTs. By the time the last Pacer journey in the North West took place on 27th November, 2020, the oldest ones on the line were 35 years old — you could buy a younger Ford Capri. (The last journey by a Pacer on that day was the 16:36 from Manchester Victoria to Kirkby.

I was between jobs at the time so not commuting to Manchester, like I had been, but it was usually the train I caught home — though the true Pacer experience would have been lost on those passengers because coronavirus-related work from home measures meant the trains were much quieter at the time. In pre-covid times, the hot oil smell was usually supplemented with a mixture of Greggs and body odour, perhaps a stale can of open Carling left in a corner and you'd have to have a mobile phone handy so you'd have somewhere to look that wasn't awkwardly into the backpack of the taller person squashed up against you because, this being the Manchester commute, there'd be no room to sit.

There are many people who would be much better qualified to talk about Pacer trains than I am, and I won't bore with too many details, but these smelly, slow and rugged trains have a place in my heart because they carried me to two things which became loves in my life. Journalism and my wife.

This is a love story, if not *that* kind of love story. But when you're trying to explain your love for a heap of metal that you bang your head on and which drains your bank account (the car), some credit needs to be given to the woman who loves you in spite of your life choices.

I'll do my best not to lose you, but before you slam this book shut and go to put the kettle on, trust me when I say that this meeting is very relevant to the future of my relationship with cars.

It was the first night of journalism school in Manchester and I was already sitting in place. I'm usually early. I looked up when the door opened and she was wearing knee-high boots and black jeans. I saw flowing hair and a beautiful face and forgot why I was in the room in the first place on that early September evening.

She'll tell you she doesn't remember the first time she saw me and she'll be telling you the truth.

By the November we'd formed a habit of being the last two remaining on post-class nights out and our first kiss was just before Christmas. By February, we were living together, though we refused to put a label on it and my dad took the piss.

The bits you don't need to know is that I would never have passed my exams if it wasn't for the teaching from my more intelligent housemate and the bit which moves this story along happened a month after our course finished.

In July 2013, my sister married the drummer.

She joked there was a 'no ring, no bring' policy, but there are clear pictures of me with my plus-one, so I must have been made an exception.

On their way to winning the rugby league Challenge Cup that year, Wigan Warriors beat London Broncos 70-0 in a semi-final on the day of the wedding but my interests were placed elsewhere.

Vintage buses.

They have a feel to them. The click of shoes on the floor, the steepness of the stairs, the fag burns in seats, the *thugg-a-guggg* of the idling engine.

We were on such a bus. When I say 'we', this is me, mum, dad, and my future wife, though at the time I'm sure I hoped more than she did that this would be the case.

The wood, the oil, the smell, the noise — I was a child again, at a museum or at a motorshow in Ormskirk, seeing how happy my dad was. I wanted to be in the driving seat.

We watched my sister marry the drummer and I was responsible for the music. I hit the play button too early and had to pause it, and then had to start the music again, which I think annoyed the drummer. But my little brother stole the show with his reading and then I stumbled through mine before the next awakening hit of car fever.

The happy couple left the scene in a blue Morris Minor (more on those later) and I was prepared to happily toddle to the bus before dad intervened.

He had hired, I'm sure for himself, a Daimler DS420 limousine to take him, my mum and, as it turns out, me and my plus-one back to the reception.

The earliest DS420s are from 1968 and if you were using a description that my dad's dad might have employed, they are 'well appointed.'

They are basically like a Jaguar with an extended floorpan, with room for six passengers, three of which travel on fold-up 'occasional seats' while the others use a permanent bench seat. Last into the car, I slid across the leather and feeling such an old car in a 'live' state gave me a pang.

It had been ten years since dad and I gave up on that fuel pump. I wanted to try again.

10

A (big) Bump in the Road

2007 Fiat Punto
'Edith' was a blue Fiat Punto with a replacement engine and 120,000 miles on the clock by the time we'd run her into the ground. We bought her from my girlfriend's sister so I could teach her to drive in it. I say teach, she had a few lessons from years previous under her belt and a couple of failed tests, so it was time to start again.

My wife and I didn't start off in the most conventional of ways, it must be said. We moved into a flat together while we were studying to become journalists before we were official. Dad loved taking the piss out of us being 'friends.'

Her first meeting with my dad was unfair on my part. I thought it would be a nice idea to take her for a walk near where I grew up. There are woods and a little hill called Billinge Lump by locals. It's the highest point in Merseyside and forms the western part of the Douglas Valley. To the east, you can see Rivington, Manchester, Bolton and Wigan, following to Pendle at the north. Then there's Blackpool (including the tower on a clear day) as you come round to the east, Southport, Liverpool, the sea and North Wales when you start to come south before Widnes and the Runcorn Bridge. In the right light you can see Jodrell Bank before you loop back around to Manchester. It's honestly lovely. I spent a lot of time in my youth walking up there for the view — sometimes early enough to watch the sun come up – and smoke without being caught.

I pulled the car up on my parents' drive thinking no-one would be in and thought that I was right until I heard my dad's Insignia coming around the corner. He wound the window down and shouted 'Sophie!' without being introduced. He was very excited to meet her, so our walk would have to wait. Inside, my mum was being my mum and trying to sort something out with the Post Office online, so the first word Sophie heard my mum say was 'wanker' at a volume which would have made birds leave their trees three miles away.

Something went alright though, as she came on the walk with me, even though we saw two tenths of fuck all at the top of the lump because it was misty. It was also wet — she slipped in the mud — but somehow things progressed, possibly more smoothly than they would have done if she knew it would result in living with a permanent oil stain on the drive.

We started out in a flat in Wigan, close enough to walk to the train station for Sophie's job in Manchester and for town centre pubs at the weekends. I kept the Corsa for my job doing admin for one of the departments at the council while we carried on with our training.

Sophie needed wheels though — especially as a requirement for most journalism jobs is access to a car. Luckily, her sister had just what we needed, a cheap Fiat Punto with a shedload of miles on it. Almost 100,000 to be more accurate. All we had to do was pick it up from her home, which was 200 miles away.

The Punto felt very different to the Corsa in every way. It felt wider, had less power — it felt 'plastic-y.' The first time I drove it was the mile-eating trip back to Wigan from the Midlands where it lived, taking the A50 until it joins the M6 at Stoke.

After getting used to it, the drive seemed fine.

That is, until I buggered-up the lanes on the three-lane roundabout near Stoke City's ground and caused a van driver to lean on the horn and give me a gesture that suggested I spent a bit too much personal time in the bathroom. This made me nervous and I found myself in the outside lane of the M6 sliproad being tailgated by an old couple in a hilarious reversal of stereotypical roles while said van undertook us with the window wound-down and more signed suggestions on what I should do with myself. Not great driving on my part, and it has caused me to revisit that roundabout since to get it right and exorcise those demons.

We practised every night. From the car park at the flat, Sophie would supplement her driving lessons with extras from me after a first re-acquaintance with being on the right hand side of the car on a quiet industrial estate road.

After pulling in and swapping over, I could hear my dad's voice in my head telling me what to do as I went through the process with my 'friend.' In fairness, she already knew about putting the car into gear, biting points and checking mirrors, but I doubted the refresher would have hurt as we pulled away and I don't recall as much juddering as when I kangaroo-hopped the Corsa around Skelmersdale.

Over the weeks that followed, as lingering summer evenings gave way to darker and wetter nights, we didn't let the regime slip, despite the bickering that can come with being given guidance by a partner when negotiating bus lanes in Bolton, or being at the front of the queue at traffic lights on the East Lancashire Road.

I like to think it was my tutelage, but it's more likely Sophie's professional driving instructor had more to do with the fact she passed on the first attempt since she was a teenager. Edith, as the car was known, was pressed into service shortly afterwards as our journalism training gave way to jobs on local papers. The *Leigh Journal* for Sophie and a gig on the sports desk of the *Wigan Post* for me.

Things were looking good.

I'd joined a local paper at possibly the best time because 2013 in Wigan is unlikely to repeat itself. I sat at my new desk two weeks after Wigan Athletic had just won the FA Cup. Their subsequent relegation from the Premier League didn't really dilute the euphoria of that achievement. I wasn't at the final, though, something I still regret. I was taking my training very seriously and we always had classes on a Saturday. Even though I was offered a job before I had officially finished training, there was a sub-editing exam still to go, too, and this would be a big part of my job. I'd watched Wigan's semi-final win over Millwall in the bar at Manchester Piccadilly train station and, for the final, had encouraged Sophie and a friend from the course, now-football writer Richard Garnett, to join me for the final at the Piccadilly Tavern, which was a few doors down from where we were studying.

Last-minute feedback from a tutor had never been more unwelcome as he really didn't understand this was not about football — it was bigger. Edging towards the door, hints became less subtle by the second until he asked what our plans were and I said, 'Wigan are in the FA Cup final and it's kicking off... now.' I put my phone back in my pocket after using it as a prop to demonstrate the time. Could after-class feedback not wait, just this once?

I could picture the bar, rammed with nowhere to sit or see a screen. I imagined hordes of Manchester City fans which would mean my allegiances would have to remain private throughout. There would be no time to smoke as I hot-footed it to the bar. There wasn't even time to avoid cracks in the pavement or ensure each foot touched the same paving slab the same number of times.

It was mercifully quiet in the pub — cheerfully cheap and close to where we studied, we used it as a post-Saturday classes drinks venue on a weekly basis. The reassuring sound of football on the telly didn't drown-out the sounds of conversations and glasses clinking in the sporadic crowd and there were plenty of tables. Trying to get accustomed to what I'd missed in the opening four minutes, the others went to the bar while I soon became engrossed.

Keeping your allegiances to yourself when Wigan are playing against a team from Manchester in an FA Cup final, when you're in a pub in Manchester, was perhaps a little more difficult than I had thought it would be. I may be remembering it all wrong, and I've not watched the match back since, but I recall thinking to myself 'Wigan are going to win this,' as they just looked the more likely side to score throughout. It worried me, but at the same time Wigan had nothing to lose; it was just the looming threat of extra-time, which I thought would be the eventual undoing of the dream.

I don't remember if I nursed pints or watched the floor in nervous anticipation. I do remember there must have been a moment which tweaked my nerves because I heard a voice from a table behind us on which four blokes were sinking Strongbow. I'm sure I heard the words 'supporting Wigan' in an accusatory tone. Another moment of poetic torment followed — a shot which might have shaved the post or a breakthrough, I'd be lying if I said I remembered — had the rest of the pub gasping. It was a Wigan moment. The rest of the pub were also supporting them.

Never had anyone in the history of the universe been happier to be surrounded by Manchester United supporters. The table of four left and I felt safe. I began to lose myself and let myself lean and sway and give way to sharp intakes of breath at every moment as the clock ticked towards full-time and what would lead to sympathetic pats on the shoulder and quiet reflection along the lines of being proud because 'we've come this far.'

That moment never came though. Ben Watson's head has since become part of football folklore. I don't remember the corner and I don't really remember the ball going in the net. I do remember my chair falling backwards as I jumped out of it and Richard hugged me. The rest of the pub cheered and my journalism career was set — I had a reference point for dozens of articles, and having written for the paper's preview supplements, a box of keepsake bylines which all new journalists keep until at least a few years later when a clearout makes way for much-needed loft space.

Wigan's rugby league club, the Warriors, also won the Challenge Cup and Super League Grand Finals that year, making it an unreal place to work. Everyone was buzzing, and we put in shifts making supplements and magazines while eating bowls of cereal at laptops on kitchen tables until late at night. I didn't mind though, I was writing the first draft of some of Wigan's sporting history. I was made-up to be part of it.

My dad was proud. He'd comment on articles I'd written, asking about my training and telling me which bits of match reports he liked ('I've never read "penalised for mucking about at the play-the-ball" before.') and he'd suggest names of people he knew for local features when my anxiety led me to believe I wouldn't be able to bring ideas to the table.

But life was about to be knocked onto a different course by a seismic event.

*****

I'd always feared it would happen to us one day. My dad, for everything that was wonderful about him, was a heavy smoker. Not quite using a fag end to light the next one... but not far off.

I'm lucky to have nice memories of him, but there are also not nice memories. I'd lie awake at night when I was a child and listen to him coughing. A heavy smoker's cough takes on a haunting quality through two closed doors in the middle of the night and it was bad for as long as I can remember.

A very strong memory from school — I know I was eight years old, because of the playground we were in when I cried — was when a portable cabin was set-up in the car park and we sat on the carpet tiles to watch a video about smoking. I descended the steps back into daylight convinced my dad would die imminently. A lad asked me what was up and reassured me his dad had given-up and mine would too. Mustering a little bit of false hope I tried to get on with our game of football — we had to use a sponge ball because of injuries (mostly bumps to the head requiring the use of wet paper towels) caused to non-footballers who got in the way. Deep down I knew he wouldn't quit — and when you're an eight-year-old with a need to knock seven shades of shit out of a ball, a sponge one won't do.

Fast forward 18 years and my dad was in Whiston Hospital because he had heart failure. I don't remember being told he was in hospital and I don't remember how ill he was before that day in September. And I can't tell you what date it was either. I've spoken to my mum about it since, though, and apparently the August was pretty horrendous. He would lean out of an upstairs window for fresh air and couldn't walk very far.

What I do remember clearly is regular hospital visits, weaving through 'the back way'. The back way to Whiston Hospital from ours is pretty country roads that are fun to fling a Corsa around between Billinge and St Helens before going on to the hospital. I always drive up Crank Road, past my local pub, the Holts Arms (Billingers call it 'The Foot', due to its location at the foot of the hill) and over Shaley Brow — a steep hill which is more fun to drive up than down.

Going down, Billinge Lump is on your left — I'd argue it's the last Pennine — though this is a title I have given it and is by no means official (see the part about the foggy walk with Sophie for what you can see up there).

After this you go through Crank, past the notoriously, perpetually snarled-up Windle Island lights and then on to Whiston. Windle Island is near a posh bit of St Helens called Dentons Green and St Helens rugby league team train at Cowley School, where my dad once taught and his mum was a governor, which is nearby.

My description of the journey is only loosely related to cars and that, I suppose, is because I'm delaying having to type what happened the following February as I sit, seven years and nine months after the event, on a train between Manchester Victoria and Wigan after a late stop at work in November 2021.

Initially we were all very hopeful that my dad would be fine. Or as fine as you can be after open heart surgery at the age of 58 following 40-plus years of smoking close to 60 a day. (This sounds bitter but I can assure you I'm not. Everyone has faults – Christ I have them – and I loved my dad fiercely with, not despite, them).

The plan was for my dad to bin the fags and booze (a detail I've left out is that my dad had a penchant for a little bottle of scotch on a regular basis. I can hear his voice very clearly when I'm at the local shop asking for '20 Bensons and a baby Prince Consort, please.')

He'd have surgery to get a new heart valve. He would have synthetic, which would last forever, or a pig's one which would last 20 years maximum. The surgeon said there was no point going for the synthetic one because he wouldn't live 20 years, but I think we'd all have been both gobsmacked and ecstatic to see him reach 70. I'd have taken 59 in hindsight.

He never got well enough to have surgery. He was allowed to spend Christmas at home and we did what we always did — though I still haven't forgiven myself for asking him to drive to a nearby village and drop me off to meet my cousins for drinks on Christmas Eve. There's irony in a conversation I had with my aunt, over a cigarette, in which she tried to reassure me. We went to dad's dad's house for Christmas dinner and there were the usual mountains of presents, but a lack of the careless and nostalgic happiness from years previous. Deep down, I think we all knew this was the last one as a complete family unit.

What's strange is that I believed very strongly for a while that my dad would at least get better enough to have his surgery. When he was allowed home Sophie and I drove him to pick up takeaway pizza on one of the weekend nights when we nestled in at my parents' — and I wasn't strong enough to muster more than a minor protest when he sparked-up outside the takeaway. He wasn't smoking as much, but he had his secret stash, much like I had mine when I was at home, and it was suddenly clear to me that no amount of hiding packets in sock drawers, or Lynx body spray, would cover-up a secret smoker's tracks.

But after that Christmas hope started to fade. My dad became incoherent when we were visiting him, though he had moments of being with it enough to post some funny Facebook status updates. Sadly, these have since been lost as we had to get his account deleted after his death due to some bot-like status updates. It's a shame because I found trawling through his social media updates quite therapeutic.

With dad's clouded state of mind came odd phone calls in the middle of the night. He called me once to come and get him out because he said they were trapping him against his will.

'You need to come and say you're an investigative reporter for the *Wigan Post*, and if they don't let me out you'll expose them.'

I lied and said I'd come, then I cuddled into Sophie and cried. That was the moment I really knew he was going to die.

Determined to spark conversation with my dad, I still dutifully brought his *Daily Mail* (in spite of my own feelings) and tried to talk to him about what was within the pages.

On that note about feelings towards the *Mail*, I am actually a believer in reading as varied a selection of news brands as possible. It's not just because of my job as a journalist and journalism tutor. I have always felt that it is important to read news from all angles, including those that don't sit well with your personal beliefs, to give yourself the best chance of informing your own opinion. It is also important to acknowledge that you can change your opinion, and agree with individual opinions of someone whose views don't normally marry-up with your own. I feel that people should examine their opinions and beat them with a cricket bat to see how you really feel. On the subject of news brands and social media, whether angles come from the left, right or centre I'm also a big believer in everyone's opinion being given space. But it's your responsibility to decide for yourself how to broadcast them and respond to others.

The last things I bought for my dad were two car magazines that were never read. A copy of *Practical Classics* and *Classic and Sports Car*, two magazines at opposing ends of the classic car spectrum. *Practical Classics* caters for enthusiasts who don't have bespoke watches and *Classic and Sports Car* carries articles about rare Jaguars and adverts for bespoke watches. I still have the receipt in my wallet, but it has faded so much I had to look-up the date by going back nearly eight years in my bank statements.

What I can still read is that I spent £7.90 and I used my credit card, which shows I was skint through all the takeaways and hospital parking.

One date I'll never forget is Tuesday 11th February, 2014. Tuesday mornings were the deadline for the *Wigan Observer*, the weekly paper in the stable I worked for. We had 11 pages of sport each week, and I was eight months into a job I adored despite what was going on at home. I took it very seriously and loved being responsible for what my sports editor, Phil Wilkinson, and I referred to as Wigan's 'first draft of history.' Even now I still love looking through old newspapers. Adverts, in particular, really show what life was like. Those bungalows on the way into town — they were £1,500 to buy new in the mid-1960s.

Anyway, it was early morning and we were cracking on with the *Obby* when my phone went off. It was mum. I'd got to the point where my heart would sink at every call — this is the one. And this time it was. Well, nearly. I needed to go and see dad today; it wasn't good.

'Ok mum, I'll be there in a few hours.'

I walked over to the editor's desk, an amazing person called Janet Wilson, and told her I'd see the *Obby* off and leave to see my dad at noon, if that was okay. Of course it was okay. And of course I didn't tell her how bad things were. She'd have sent me on my way then if she knew.

It might seem strange to settle back to work, but immersing myself in it was a coping mechanism. If I was pre-occupied with page layouts and correcting typos I wasn't getting upset. The phone went again.

'Come now. Hospital have been on the phone. It's really not good.'

I arrived at Whiston at lunchtime and navigated the ramps and tight spaces in the multi-storey like Colin McRae. No time for waiting for the lift; I wouldn't be surprised if my heels loosened the plaster underneath the stairs as I flew down them two at a time.

Hospital sounds were augmented. Squeaky shoes on polished floors. The *shudunk* of automatic doors. The mechanical whirr of the hand sanitiser dispenser in an era when they only existed in such places. I knew the way to the ward and arrived there in a trance, like when you don't remember driving home.

We were at the stage in visiting my dad when you'd just say hello into the intercom and they'd buzz you in outside of visiting hours. You get to do that when you've got a family member who is dying, and you know you have been promoted to that group when nurses bring you coffee and toast. They give you a look; it's oddly reassuring.

My mum and my siblings were in a side room. They give you

the side room when you're really in the shit. No one was crying, but it was very quiet. I accepted the offer of coffee because even though people tend not to eat and drink in such circumstances, it isn't going to change anything if you do and I drink coffee like there is no tomorrow which, for my dad, there wouldn't be.

Waiting for someone to die is really odd. I don't know what it's like for other people, but I didn't get upset. I just went into crisis management mode. I'm the sort of person who will have a meltdown over a broken cupboard door, but if the roof blows off the house I become a general and take control.

My dad wasn't lucid, but he wasn't asleep. After asking for the curtain to be pulled across I just sat and held his hand. I don't know if he could hear me but I told him I loved him just in case. I'm happy we were never embarrassed to say or show that and I hope the same for my sons now. The car magazines were still on the table, quite untouched.

I won't say we were all raised Catholic, because we didn't go to church and were a sweary household. We had other things to fill Sundays with, such as rugby league and drama classes, but we went to Catholic school and as such were instilled with Catholic guilt, a knowledge of most hymns and the nagging feeling that there might be someone watching and judging when we smoke, swear, get angry, have sex before marriage or steal a chocolate from a colleague's tub of 'Miniature Heroes'.

As such, we were given the priest to give my dad the last rites and accepted that as an insurance policy. I'm sure if there is a heaven, a man like my dad would be allowed in for a multitude of reasons ranging from the number of St Helens teenagers he helped through his job to bringing life to the party. But I elected to let the priest into our bubble for five minutes just in case the sacrament was the passport he needed when he reached the queue to see St Peter.

That's what Catholic school does to you.

Eventually, the nurses moved my dad into a private room. It's uncomfortable when, during visiting hours, you're in the group with the person who is dying. It must be worse for other visitors, and I don't remember fully why but know I went outside at some point because it was dark and it snowed. It must have been to meet Sophie in the car park as she made her way over after her shift at the *Leigh Journal*.

By this point the machines blipping and beeping by my dad's bed had been turned off and the little TV that you top-up with a card like a noughties pay-as-you-go phone had gone quiet and was showing only the time on the screen.

In a quiet moment we were all around his bed and, clear as day, he opened his eyes and must have sensed we were all emotional.

'What's up?'

His enquiry broke the silence with a few laughs and was delivered in the same pitch you'd ask a toddler sitting on the kitchen floor when the dog has eaten their snack.

As time ticked on and my dad's breathing changed we insisted people start to go home. And before long, just like when my little brother was a baby, it was just me and my mum.

The three of us sitting in the semi-darkness. My mum and I reminisced, and sometimes I left my mum to talk to my dad.

Late into the evening I ventured out of my dad's room on the ground floor to the Selecta vending machines on the fifth for two bottles of pop and a very expensive sandwich in plastic packaging. It was the first time I'd been on my own for as long as I could remember, and I looked out of the huge windows over the shimmering yellow lights stretching to the horizon. Traffic was sparse and as I was the only one up there the corridors were dark until my presence was close enough to trigger the lights on. It was like a zombie film.

I can't recall what I was thinking, but remember I couldn't cry. I don't know if my emotions were too strong to let me or if I was tired, but after a few minutes I decided I would hurry back. I couldn't decide if it was better for my mum to be alone with my dad when he died or not. Selfishly I wanted to be there. Unselfishly I wanted to be with my mum to support her, but I also couldn't decide if she'd prefer to be the only one there, just her and my dad, like it had been at the start.

I decided to go back downstairs and let fate decide, and when I was buzzed in, my mum was still holding my dad's hand and he was still breathing. It would be the three of us.

Loads of people have to watch their parents part ways. In my experience with peers it was usually because of divorce, and weirdly a small part of me envied those people because in many ways I felt it must have been easier than this, but at the same time I was in awe of my parents' relationship and how I was actually very lucky to be in a household which, while not always perfect, had always been loving.

'It's been a blast.'

My mum talking to my dad. If that's not something to aim for in your own relationship, I don't know what is.

*****

My dad died at eight minutes past one on the morning of 12th February 2014.

My mum and I were in the room with him. I was sitting in the big blue chair you get next to every hospital bed; this one was on my dad's left hand side, and my mum sat in a smaller chair to his right, holding his hand.

I'd never heard a death rattle before. I looked at the clock on my dad's TV, mentally noted the time, and then stood at the foot of the bed, frozen. I was useless.

My mum went to ask for the nurse and all I remember is that she told my mum to hold his hand. She was brilliant and I don't know her name and that's a shame. My mum did as she said and it calmed her.

We didn't hang around. My mum wanted to leave my dad while he was still warm, so I called Sophie to tell her and took my mum to the Corsa.

It was clear and cold. I love February skies and there were thousands of stars and it seemed like we were the only people out. I didn't know what to feel or think.

I just knew that life was going to be very different.

11

Plan MGB

1979 MGB GT
The MGB comes as a soft-top and the hard-top MGBGT, which was a Pininfarina design that is beautiful to look at.

MGBs are one of the more common exhibits at classic car shows and with a good reason — they're accessible, reasonable to run (as far as classics go) and are decent cars.

I always wanted one and had to have one. It had to be orange.

Perhaps it was grief but in the months after my dad's death my car obsession grew. Since I was small I'd wanted an MGB GT — basically an MGB with a hard-top — and it must be orange.

Much like the Midget, the MGB evolved a lot during its near-18-year production run, 1962 to 1979. Chrome bumpers were replaced by heavy plastic ones in the mid-70s to comply with US safety regulations, and despite the fact US exports of the GT stopped in 1974, the rubber bumper styling stayed.

Like the Midgets of the same era, there isn't much love for rubber-bumpered MGBs, and also like Midgets, these are the MGBs I love the most. I knew from the start — that is, when I was a child — that mine had to be a rubber bumper model and it also had to show some battle scars. I wasn't interested in a show winner. The odd scratch and dent was fine by me, I wanted something to drive every day.

I spent most of my spare time, and a lot of work's time, looking through ads and websites at what would suit my budget. The big advantage I had was that what I wanted — and in the state I wanted it — would be cheap.

I really should have slowed down a bit when my dad died. My tears came at around five o'clock in the morning after we'd driven home from the hospital and I was wrongly worrying about work already. But I knew I had to take a step back, despite my sports editor being away in Australia for Wigan Warriors' World Club Challenge match against Sydney Roosters.

English clubs actually have a pretty good record in that, staged annually (or at least it's supposed to be) between Super League's best and the NRL champions down under. One day that might mean a battle between French and New Zealand sides, though so far a competition that has been staged since 1976 on and off, mainly off, has meant England v Australia. Critics will tell you that so much English success is down to the match usually being played on a freezing February UK night, with a further claim that the Aussie clubs don't take it seriously, seeing it as a pre-season warm-up. If you'd have asked me when I was younger, or three years later when I saw Wigan win it, I'd have argued with you and defended the concept, but I can see both sides these days.

On this occasion Wigan, the only British team to win one of these matches in Australia until St Helens did it in 2023, decided they would try to emulate probably their best ever side from 20 years previous by doing it again. They would face the Roosters, in Sydney, on 22nd February.

They, and my boss, were already in the Southern Hemisphere with Wigan set to meet NZ Warriors – another NRL team – on the morning of my dad's death. My intention was to watch that game for a distraction, but having been awake for so long I slept until well after the full-time whistle. Wigan won their warm-up and with a huge week ahead for the paper I didn't want to let my colleagues down. I was in the office the following Monday.

Keeping busy was a self-preservation tactic that I thought worked well at the time, but in hindsight it delayed my grief, which trickled out in bits over a longer period of time.

Come the big match in Sydney, Wigan were soundly beaten by a better side, but away from rugby my search for a car was on, and in the spring I thought I'd found the perfect one. My plan was to combine a small pot of savings and funds from selling my Corsa, and there was an orange BGT in St Helens for just over two grand – my plan was to offer two on the nose.

I *umm*-ed and *ahh*-ed while getting insurance quotes, read up on what they are like as a 'daily' (doable, but be prepared to learn how to deal with electrical faults when it rains and, as always, rust is the enemy). I sought advice from everyone I spoke to, and it got to the point where my mum told me to hold off and Sophie was telling me to just go and buy it so I'd stop incessantly talking about it. I called the number.

I'd missed my chance by a few days. The owner was after a quick sale and in the end it had gone to a dealer for £1,500.

'I'd have snatched your hand off for two, mate,' was no consolation, but perhaps it wasn't to be. The same car appeared a few weeks later on the dealer's website for a considerable mark-up and looking shinier in better photos. There was no chance of a reduction in price despite me calling them to say I knew how much they had paid for it.

My next target was another orange B GT for sale near Chorley, a couple of junctions up from me on the M6. It was going for a couple of grand more than the previous one I had looked at, and as it would go over my budget I was unsure. My mum came with me when I went to have a look, and we just about managed to find it when I was trundling around a maze of streets and the sun gleaming off a polished bit of orange front wing caught my eye. I was about to drive an MG for the first time.

With the owner in the passenger seat I was even more nervous than I otherwise would be – and that was a lot. Adjusting the seat was the first challenge, I'm not the tallest person to say the least and my toes could barely touch the pedals when I first clambered in to sit in the 'deckchair' patterned cloth seat. That was another feature I was after as well as the rubber bumpers and the orange — a lot of these seats were swapped out for vinyl on B GTs, but there's something about the original and disgusting seats I really liked.

Proving I was a complete novice, there was no chance of faking it as I was then shown how to use the choke to get the car started, and with the wobbliest, most nervous lift off the clutch I had ever performed, we just about rolled off the drive and I experienced what it's like to manoeuvre a car without power-steering for the first time. There was a concrete fence which seemed like inches in front of us, a parked car to our right, and I'm sure the owner of this precious vehicle was doing everything in his power not to let his instincts overcome him and grab hold of the wheel.

I only drove to the end of the road before we turned around and I crunched the gears looking for reverse before dry-steering my way out of the turn. The ordeal must have lasted maybe three minutes, but it was horrendous. I think both of us in the car knew that I wasn't going to be driving home in it, and in a rare case of seller trying to put off buyer, he suggested making a 36-year-old car do the daily run to work wasn't fair on it. Feeling rather flat, I got back into the nine-year-old Corsa and drove home, though I took a few minutes to re-adjust as now the Vauxhall's steering felt ultra light and the brakes ultra efficient. My poor mum hadn't been driven as badly since she went out with me in the Agila when I was learning.

I wasn't put off though. Maybe it was just that an MGB wasn't quite the best first classic for me, despite everything I'd read saying they were ideal to get started on.

I knew as much as I didn't want what's known as a 'wash and go' classic. These are basically cars from the late '80s through to the '90s which had status at the time, such as a Peugeot 205 or a VW Golf, or something which has since become trendy like a Rover 75 or Renault Clio. These all have their place and are rightly adored by their enthusiasts, but if I were to go for a car from this era I had my heart set on a Mini.

The first BMW Minis, still called the 'new' Minis by a lot of people, were first on the road in 2001. Now, the first ones fall into this bracket of a 'wash and go' classic, but despite being cheaper to buy these aren't the Minis I was interested in. However, Minis are hard to shop for.

My earliest Mini memory was my dad sitting in one in a showroom and I must have been very young because I can't find a reference point to date the event. Usually a song on the radio, the shoes my sister had at the time, a coat or which car we were in provides me with some sort of clue as to when something happened. I'm sure it's the same for other people, but I have a decent knack of knowing the year of a film or a song not because I've done any sort of revision but because I am good at filing memories from about 1993 to 2001. The early noughties are a bit blurry and then from 2006 the clarity returns.

Oddly, that gap is about the same length of time as a dip in my interest in rugby league, which tells me I use that a lot in my mental filing system.

So, I must have been six or a bit younger.

My dad wasn't the tallest person in the world — he was bang on six feet — and he sat in the driver's seat of the Mini and hardly fit. I think he might have been having a laugh because he drove plenty of Midgets and I've since seen taller people drive Minis. Anyway, we didn't get one.

In my experience, looking for a reasonably-priced Mini which hasn't been modified is basically impossible.

You can forget really classic examples, which are crazy money. There's a beautiful green Mini that lives near me which would be a dream car to own, but even if its doting owner were ever to sell the thing, it would be beyond my means. If you gave me a free shot at the perfect Mini it would be any example from the '60s, as long as it's blue with a white circle for a racing number, but with no number in it. I will unashamedly admit it's because that was the Mini motor racer James Hunt drove, but these aren't the cars I grew-up with.

The right one for me was parked under my nose.

12

Midgeteering

1979 MG Midget
Built between 1962 and 1979 (the last few were registered in 1980), the MG Midget has a dedicated fan base, but it is unlikely to top the wishlist of many lottery winners.

As the name suggests, they are tiny. You know about it where you're sharing the road with Chelsea Tractors and vans, but doing 30mph feels like 50mph. I've never had as much fun driving a car as I have in my Midget.

The last version of the Midget, the 1500, was introduced in 1974 and plagued by having to comply with US safety regulations which brought with it an increased ride height and heavy plastic bumpers (known as rubber bumpers), both making it handle like a broken shopping trolley. People tend not to like this incarnation of the Midget, but it's the one I grew-up with and the one I love the most.

It was my mum who suggested I look for a Midget, if I was still hell-bent on having a classic and, despite the shaky experience in the BGT, I was.

They were slightly more budget-friendly than Bs, but the sticking point was that without a specialist hardtop, if I were to stick with my plan of using one as a daily driver I would have to rely on a vinyl hood to keep out horizontal rain — and looking back it was madness to drive a Midget to work in the depths of winter. Before I would consider this aspect though, there was no thinking time; I hadn't even thumbed a printed classified section in *Classic Car Weekly* before I found it online. It might even have been my first day of looking.

In Wigan, on budget, was a red Midget. I called straight away to make sure it was available and was on my way to an estate in Platt Bridge within hours.

As usual when coming to view a car, it was out on the drive and visible from down the street as I pulled-up in the Corsa, negating the need to crawl past each house looking for a number on the door. I was thrilled to see the red car in the photos was actually the same orange as the BGT I had viewed before. *The orange I was desperate for my car to be.* It was already mine, but I had to take it on what I feared was going to be another nervy test run.

Even as a kid, getting in — and even more so getting out of — a Midget is not something which can be done with much dignity, and as I've got older the problem only gets worse. I'm only 5ft 8in, not what you'd exactly describe as a robust person. But once you've clicked the chrome handle and swung the tiny door open, the unmistakeable squidging sound of denim on vinyl prolongs embarrassment while you try and unhinge your right leg to get it into the car and planted in the footwell. There's loads of room once you're in, but F1 drivers have less work to do when boarding their vehicles. I was expecting the worst as the seller got in next to me, the car already running.

Weirdly I felt at ease as I carefully lifted the clutch, taking the little car onto the quiet residential road. Even though I knew what travelling in a Midget was like, I had never done it on the right hand side of the car, and I hadn't been on the road in one for 15 years. The first thing that strikes you is how small and vulnerable you feel at first, even with no other cars around.

But happily the driving experience, for me, was much better than when I tested the B. I'm not sure if I'd feel the same today — I'm much more used to driving classic cars now. Maybe it's an experience or a confidence thing. Driving the Midget was like driving a go-kart. Even just bumbling around the housing estate at about 20mph was the most fun I'd had in a car. A lot gets said about rubber bumpered Midgets built at a time when British Leyland wasn't exactly renowned for quality, but I was none-the-wiser. It was brilliant and I was hooked. The formality of making an offer was done quickly, and we shook hands on £2,000 – all I had to do was come back with Sophie in her car so I could drive home and discover what I was really letting myself in for.

Through my own excitement I still noticed a sadness in the seller's demeanour when I returned with Sophie in her Punto to pay for and take the Midget — which I'd already christened 'Midge' — home. We were in the front room while I transferred the money on my phone, me overlooking a small crusty patch where the rear wing joined the bumper, a fuel gauge which wasn't showing a reading and a less than perfect hood. Neither of us sat down while I pinged the money across and, with the car, I was given a green file with a detailed history dating back to the '90s. A previous owner had been meticulous in documenting every service and repair, and I found out they'd called the car Ellie. I wasn't having that — from now on it was Midge as I carried on our family tradition of being unimaginative when naming cars.

It also felt a little bit like fate, if you go for that sort of thing, in that Midge was registered in Rutland — the smallest county in the country when the tide is in and where Sophie is from.

The drive to our flat in the town centre was really short, so I'd told Sophie to head home and I'd call her if I got really stuck. With a wave, the seller closed the front door while I sat in my MG on the drive. I was on my own with a 35-year-old car and about to drive solo in traffic. I didn't know how to categorise my emotions, but I was too nervous to shake. I pulled out the choke and turned the key.

About five minutes later I found myself knocking on the door, having not moved apart from to clamber unceremoniously back out of the car. I needed a hand getting the car started. It wasn't that I didn't understand the mechanics of what I had to do — I knew I'd need to pull out the choke — but I wasn't getting any more than a sound that would become a familiar feature of my life from here, an engine turning over but firing up.

The former keeper of my car got in and performed some sort of witchcraft and the car sprang into life. There wasn't much to it, I was to learn, but at the time it felt like I was trying to steal Biff Tannen's 1946 Ford Coupe in *Back to the Future* ('No one can start that car but me') and if I couldn't get it started, how was I going to do things like service it, repair it, drive it safely? One problem at a time.

I was still driving very slowly as I started to leave the housing estate and approach the main road. My saving grace was that my very first turn to join actual traffic while driving an MG would be to the left, meaning there'd be less pressure to get away quickly, less chance of stalling and less chance of becoming stranded. Then the first shock to the system when driving an older car rushed towards me as if I was doing 70mph instead of 5mph.

After a while you get used to swapping between modern and classic cars and the differences are less surprising the more you do it, but the very first time you press the brake pedal in an old car and expect to stop straight away is a scary one. It's not that these brakes don't work or are unsafe, they just work differently and require a different technique for coming to a halt. A gentle dab with your right toe won't have the same effect as it does in a new car, and that's exactly what I did at first — and thankfully I was trickling, rather than hurtling, along.

I leaned in and gave the brakes a push like an F1 driver having out-braked a rival into turn one, and the Midget dutifully came to an abrupt stop — the brakes did indeed work.

It's hard to explain what it is when getting used to things like this in a classic. With braking, lots of it is down to anticipation, and as you're never complacent because it's noisy, you're cold, conscious you're drawing attention anyway and very aware your own safety is in the hands of fewer life-saving features. In short, you become a more considerate driver.

On the other hand, I think a lot of it is also down to simply getting used to the equipment you have, because none of what I've said above can help you if you ever have to do an emergency stop in a classic car. I recall one incident near a school when I had to act quite quickly for a loose football, which might have been being chased by a child. Said football was unhurt and I was even able to wait for the child to retrieve it without stalling.

As big an issue of getting used to brakes is the fact you're on very skinny tyres when you're in a Midget. Less tyre surface area in contact with the road equals less grip, and if you get your braking wrong, especially in the wet (but don't be fooled into thinking it won't happen in the dry), you can find yourself having to arrest a little slide.

It doesn't happen often, and you quickly learn that when it does the best thing is to hold the wheel straight and feel when you need to brake — it happened twice to me during my four years with the Midget and I was lucky both times we were on quiet roads when I was driving slowly.

But my third lesson in the Midget wasn't to do with losing traction. After learning there's a knack to starting (but not what this knack is) and that the brakes felt heavy (some people overcome this by fitting a servo, a device to make the pedal feel lighter) my third lesson was how to cope with driving in the rain.

It's an experience many classic owners don't contend with because they simply won't take their cars out in anything other than the best weather — which is best for enjoyment and preservation, but unhelpful advice when you've bought a 1979 soft top for your daily commute.

The drive home was short and the rain wasn't biblical, but then a bit of drizzle is a bigger deal when you're in a Midget instead of a Corsa, and there are good points and bad points to what you have at your disposal to help you.

Your roof will probably be leaky, especially if, like mine, it is a bit past its best and has a tear in it, and because it is old and made of vinyl the sides will shave shrunk slightly, meaning there's no protection. Your windscreen is also tiny, so visibility becomes more of an issue. Wipers are also about as useful as a chocolate teapot. They have two speeds: on and on a bit faster, and they don't self-park, so you have to time when to switch them off if you're doing this mid-drive. There is also no way to operate them from the steering column, so you quickly get used to where the switch is on the dash so you can flick it on and off without looking.

The good points are your heaters. A Midget's heaters can unfreeze near-frostbitten limbs in seconds and keep a takeaway warm. There is also a metal flap in each footwell which, when opened, lets the heat of the engine work its magic on sodden jeans and upholstery, and the upholstery does get wet because the roof leaks, and if you end up in heavy enough rain the water from the road starts to come in through the holes where the pedals stick out. All this water means you also need to be very aware that you will get rust problems and you will get welding bills with your MOT. Here I should say that you really mustn't wait for an MOT to get any problems fixed because an MOT certificate isn't proof of roadworthiness — it only proves the car was roadworthy at the time of the test. And after spending so much time outside, the inevitable happened with mine as crusty bits stuck out from the parapet, or more accurately, from the floor pan.

A lot of surviving British Leyland MGs have had to undergo considerable welding work and many have given their owners terminally-ill credit cards because they have had to fork out for extensive repairs that have been hidden under layers of filler and nicely-polished paint, ignored when hearts ruled heads during the buying process.

I've heard from a few people that the '80s were the era of the bodge, and DIY repair stories have ranged from filling gaps in bodywork with newspaper and covering it with filler to welding flattened-out empty beer cars into gaps in the floor. Thankfully, I think the death-trap reputation of classics has been addressed a little in recent times with the demand for higher quality repairs and restoration work, helped by the fact these cars are older and more cherished now, though human nature undoubtedly would take over in some instances and a minimal cost approach to keeping the car on the road might well be favoured by some.

Before getting to that point though, I still had to learn how to start the thing. Choke out, turn key — nothing. Who knew how to start a Midget? My mum. The difference being hers hadn't been driven for about ten years and was in considerably better condition than mine.

'Have you given it some gas?'
'No.'
'Try pressing the throttle when you turn the key.'
Bingo.

13

Coming Home

1966 Morris Minor
Top speed: 73 mph
0—60: 16.2 seconds
Economy: 32 mpg
Engine: 1098cc, four—cylinder

You can move house with an MG Midget. I've done it twice.

Admittedly, the first time, we were only packing-up a four-room flat and moving four miles across town to a five-room cottage. I also had a Fiat Punto at my disposal and we did it in many, many trips, but you *can* move house with an MG Midget.

I wanted to be closer to my mum after my dad died and Sophie and I both wanted to live in a house instead of a flat. It didn't take long for us to find a cottage on the main road in Billinge, about 100 yards from where I was born and a little bit further from my mum.

Next door to the butcher's, and opposite the petrol station, the little white building is known to most Billingers because they have parked in front of the drive, blocking my car in. It also stands out, as the buildings around it are mostly terraces built later in the Victorian era.

The rent was a fair bit more than our flat, and my commute to work was increased by a good 40 minutes despite it only being four miles further away — while it was fun to drive the Midget more, sitting in traffic worried about overheating wasn't the way I would have chosen to spend my time in the car.

From what I think I can work out from old maps, it looks like the building was a nail maker's cottage — that was the industry in Billinge — and even though it was within a 30-second walk of a 24-hour shop, it crucially didn't have a garage, so Midge lived under a car cover on the drive. While covers go some way to protecting cars from the weather, they have a tendency to blow off in strong winds, which are usually accompanied by rain, even if you lock the strap that goes underneath the car. Another reason covers are far from perfect is that they can actually trap moisture, making the rust problem worse.

I wasn't concerned too much about that in the height of summer, though. We moved in June 2014, with items such as lamps and the thinner bookcases we owned making the trip across town in the Midget's passenger seat with the hood down, and I brought the car bug to Billinge with me as my mum and sister were about to catch it.

My sister bought a Morris Minor, a familiar friend to everyone in the classic car community and everyone else of a certain vintage.

It was designed by Alec Issigonis — the Brit-Greek automotive designer who also brought us the Mini — and had a production run from 1948 all the way to 1971. Issigonis had a habit of designing cars that stood the test of time, his Mini design was still recogniseable, in fact, barely changed from 1959 to 2000.

If you go to a car show, you will see a clutch of Moggies, and while their place in pop culture doesn't need assurance, it was given a helping hand by appearing in *Open All Hours* and by

Phyllis Crane in *Call the Midwife*. 'Me and dad had this thing where we used to see them, and like them, and talk about them a lot,' explained Kat, my sister. 'Nurse Gladys Emmanuel — it was a real talking point for us — a reference in pop culture we could talk about.'

Searching for her own answers, after I'd asked my sister to ponder why she went for a Morris Minor, she thought of another reason it had to be something as wonderfully impractical.

'One was my wedding car,' she said. 'The one that was my wedding car was the same colour. It was the last car dad and I were ever alone in.'

I never got to drive the CGL 460D before she sold it two years later, but my sister and I did manage the odd jaunt in tandem, the Minor's blue contrasting sharply with the blaze of orange that followed.

I rode shotgun with her once, on the drive home from Manchester on the day she'd bought it, and I loved everything about it. I was also jealous when she managed to fix a stuck float chamber just by reading a manual, something I could do now, but at the time simple maintenance tasks still eluded me and I was frustrated that I needed help when she could get on with it. She's like that tough, my sister. Give her something to work out and she just will.

It's true what they say about Morris Minors and the noise they make — they're the kind of cars you hear before you see them because they genuinely do parp along, and apparently the clutch takes some getting used to as it comes up from out of the floor, rather than hanging into the footwell as on most cars. She was gutted when she sold it, but admitted it could have been a grief purchase and she wasn't giving it the attention it needed.

'I hadn't time and it wasn't fair on the car,' she said. 'I had a romantic idea of what it would be like. I was in my 20s and wanted the knowledge, but I had none of the patience. I was also in the middle of my PhD and overwhelmed with other stuff.

'It was a kindness to sell it. And when the guy came to look at it and he was so over the moon, I knew it was the right thing.'

Even though she only owned a classic car for a couple of years, Kat has experience of mine and my mum's up-and-down relationship with cars, and had her fair share of experiences.

'It always fucking broke, it had tantrums,' she said. 'I'm also a carer pretty much full-time when I'm not in work, so I can't get stranded in a car.

'Mum tells horror stories of when dad had the MG BGT and she wouldn't see him because he'd broken down and had no way of contacting her.

'The Mog suffered from under use, and that led to lack of reliability. I didn't want to faff with it.

'The number of times I had to get you, Sophie and Heapy to push me down a hill...'

I've generally been very lucky as far as breakdowns are concerned. When I get caught out, I have usually managed to make it home, but Kat is able to, like most of us, look back at mishaps with a dash of romance.

'They provide you with bonding experiences,' she said. 'It's really wonderful, you look back on them fondly, but at the time you wish you'd never even thought about buying it and you question your life choices.

'But modern cars don't make good stories. No one ever told an exciting story about a Focus.'

A car never in danger of being sold though was JED, the Midget I grew-up with, and with a bit of gentle persuasion my mum decided it was time to put it back on the road after a ten-year break.

JED is special to us and because it has been kept in a garage and done relatively few miles, just shy of 30,000 for a 40-plus-year-old car, it is mostly in very good condition, we just needed to make it roadworthy again.

That job fell to a guy named Guy, who runs a business in

Wigan called GA Welding. My classic car mishaps over the years have led him to start answering the phone with an 'alright lad,' knowing my request is going to require some sort of rescue to slot into his busy schedule, but he is busy for a reason, as many people with classics in the area will attest to.

He arrived at my mum's house after work, walked up the steep drive into the garage and without any trouble got the engine turning by hand.

'Yep, we'll sort it,' he said confidently, in a thick accent my mum and Sophie can't understand.

He came back with his low loader to take JED away, and I know it was a bit of a wrench for my mum to see it leave the spot it had been resting for the past decade, but it was always going to be difficult given what the car represents and the timing. But I knew it was important we did this so she could have something happy to look forward to after months of adjusting to being without my dad.

In the end it was a relatively simple job for Guy, a recommission and a service, going over the mechanical components to make sure everything was safe, and putting it through a first MOT in just over a decade.

I remember getting the call from Guy while I was having an evening out in Manchester with Sophie. I was about four cocktails deep when he told me that the car was fixed, good news, but he was about to do the MOT and couldn't find the Vehicle Identification Number, or VIN, which is stamped on the body of the car, usually under the bonnet, and needed for MOTs. I know now that the plate it is stamped onto is at the front when you lift the bonnet, but it is hard to see because it's the same colour as the car.

At the time I didn't, though, and with the minutes ticking by until the garage closed and we'd have to wait into the next week, I did what I always do and called my mum.

Cue that trait of my mum's I mentioned earlier and which she has passed on to me, how we both have the ability to get into a flap over not very much. Nought to 100 full-flapping mode in about five seconds. But on the other hand, when there's a real crisis, such as the roof has blown off the house or we're dealing with a death in the family, we can direct proceedings with the calmness of a Supreme Court judge. This was not one of those latter moments.

Half-pissed and standing outside a bar, only half able to hear the conversations on my phone, I tried to explain to my mum that a number that I didn't know existed was missing and without it we couldn't do the MOT. On the other end of the phone I could just about make out the sound of her clunking through filing cabinets looking for the logbook and I was patting my pockets and gesticulating to Sophie for something to write it down with should she find it.

'Hang on.'

My mum's voice suddenly cut through the panic as I tried to smoke quietly enough for her not to hear on the other end of the phone.

'Tell them it's on a plate at the front when you open the bonnet. The number is black like the car, so it's hard to see.'

Neither of us know where this little nugget of information came from, but I quickly called Guy back and there it was – problem solved. I fidgeted through the rest of my cocktail while waiting to hear the results of the test, and when the call came it was back to jostling for a good enough signal to hear the news while pacing around the pavement outside, but there was no need to worry — it had passed.

I could hardly wait for work to finish on the Monday so I could walk over to the garage and take JED home to my mum. Our office at the time was on an industrial unit on the edge of town and the 20-minute walk involved going past the stadium Wigan's professional rugby league and football teams share, before taking the footbridge over the canal to another industrial estate. I had an envelope of cash in my inside jacket pocket which I kept checking while reminding myself not to be nervous. I knew how to drive these cars and it was only a short trek back to mum's; it just might be lengthened by the rush hour traffic.

You'd think on this first drive I would be heading straight for the B roads and not seen by my family for a good few hours, as I enjoyed my first drive in a car which had meant so much to me throughout my life. The reality was quite different.

Yes, I did have a huge smile on my face when I climbed in and started the car on the button, with no extra effort on my part due to sticky choke cables or applying a squeeze of the accelerator to offer encouragement.

The first thing I noticed was how lively it sounded compared to mine.

The starter motor seemed brighter and when the engine kicked in you could tell it had been put through less work. It just sounded... new. I've already talked about comparisons that can be made with a shopping trolley when discussing the handling of a late Midget, and admittedly I didn't stretch the car's 'legs' enough to find out about JED on this occasion, but what I could guess from the feel on the drive was that it would handle like a very new shopping trolley. Everything felt that little bit more assured than the worn-in character of my own car.

But I was nervous. I did start to enjoy the drive a little bit more as I neared Billinge, but wanted to get home to my mum as soon as I could. Also, driving someone else's precious possession with years' worth of sentimental value is very different to driving something of your own that you've not had much time to become very attached to. What if this car that hasn't moved in a decade breaks down? What if I have an accident? Does the fuel gauge work?

I tried to push these thoughts to the back of my mind as I paid Guy, collected the paperwork and folded the hood away properly. It was down, ready for me to enjoy the early evening sun, but hadn't been folded properly, and there's a particular way of doing it so that you can put the tonneau cover back on.

That shaky foot on the clutch returned. I had specifically worn trainers instead of the usual boots I wear to work in case this happened, but we were away without any trouble and back on the road. I was driving JED, this was amazing, and terrifying.

I managed it though, and was relieved to have made it through the traffic without any incidents and towards my mum's. I pulled over to call her and say I was minutes away, I knew that she would want to be waiting outside to see me bring her car home. We should really have gone out properly again, and I wanted to as I pulled up and told my mum to jump in. I hadn't realised at the time, but the only time she would have sat in the passenger seat in this car before now would have been with my dad driving. I think it only hit us both when we were actually moving again as I quickly drove round the block before carefully negotiating the steep drive, without any wheels slipping, and nosing it into the garage next to Maggie.

Without much space between the cars, I slithered out of the driver's seat trying not to touch the Midget's door against the Magnette. Once in an upright position, I did what I always did in the garage and poked my head in through the open driver's window of the Magnette and took in the smell of wood and old leather.

I patted the dusty roof of the car like a right saddo and then spoke to the car like an even bigger saddo.

'Not long for you.'

14

It Begins

2011 Fiat 500
With 120,000 miles on the clock, our seven-year-old Punto was looking very sorry with bumps, scrapes and a botched home paint job. Sophie's new going-to-work mobile was a little red Fiat 500. I'd obviously have preferred a more vintage edition to the 2011 version we had, but I came to enjoy this one — until it also gave us problems.

The V5C document landed on my doormat nine months and a week after my dad died. Number of former keepers, four. Last keeper, William McCooey. I was the new custodian of Maggie, officially.

I've never considered myself the owner of the ZA — four McCooey children grew up with her. It just so happens I'm the one who was probably most likely to take on putting her back on the road. My name and address is on the logbook, but Maggie belongs to all of us, I've always thought that. I'd decided before dad died that we would actually fix this car this time, and we'd follow through with the project that stalled in my teenage years when I had my head turned by guitars, beer and Bon Jovi.

Even after another decade, I was naïve about the job in front of us. I knew it would be a slow-burner because I'd need to fund it, but I had no idea how much would be involved. I also had next to no idea what I was doing.

One thing I did know was we'd need new sills on each side as they were rusted through, and at £80 for the pair added those to my initial shopping list. Furthermore, I'd have to look for someone to fit them as I'd never held a welding torch, never mind have any idea what I would be supposed to do with one.

I knew the semaphore indicators weren't working and it had starting issues — possibly down to the fuel pump, which dad and I had started to look at during the last time we were seriously thinking about getting the car on the road, but the first job was to clear three childhoods' worth of crap from in and around the interior. During her time in the garage Maggie has become a sort of dumping ground for toys, board games still in their cellophane from many Christmases gone, and items you could file under 'misc' such as office supplies, old schoolbooks and spare bits of tiles and trims from various home improvement projects over the years. Above all this in my mum's garage is what we've always called the garage loft. It's essentially a huge shelf which you could easily stand up on, even fit a double bed and a TV if you really wanted to, and that was also full of crap.

The issue I had was that I couldn't just order a skip and start filling it. Well, I could, but three quarters of the junk in this pile wasn't mine to throw away, and the quarter that was mine I didn't want to throw away for the same reasons I couldn't throw my siblings' stuff out. A boxed Tracy Island with all the *Thunderbirds* figures and rockets. A *Star Wars* Micro Machines Millennium Falcon, various games consoles and tons of games for each — yep — the stuff I wanted to 'store' at my mum's house and not throw out. As a side note, I was really very lucky to have been given the

Tracy Island in 1992. People were going mad for them to the point where *Blue Peter* even showed us how to make one out of yoghurt pots and washing-up liquid bottles. It was nowhere near my birthday or Christmas and I don't remember having done anything of note, such as string two weeks together at school or suddenly start hoovering the house. But my dad telephoned Toys 'R' Us in Warrington to reserve one for me. I don't know if you had to pay a deposit, but it seems odd that just writing someone's name on a box would stop other people taking it anyway during a time of such desperate need for injection moulded plastic in the shape of the *Thunderbirds* base. When we got there, the box with my name on it was dented, but there was another with no name on it next to it on the floor and I remember my dad picked that one up instead, because he wanted it to be in a nice box. It doesn't matter now, of course, because after all this time the box is damaged anyway, but it's funny what you remember.

Taking a ladder to the loft, it quickly became apparent that we could fix this situation quite easily. There was a lot of room because most of it had been placed at the front of the shelf, and a good portion of it was taken up by bags and bags of old car parts, which I would throw into the 500 and take home to sort through. We just needed to do some rearranging of 20- to 30-year-old toys including Furbys, Baby All Gone and as many incarnations of Monopoly as you could imagine, and it took days. But eventually I uncovered Maggie and made enough room around it to be able to access it from all sides. Without much of a clue of what I was doing, it was more of a walkaround with a cloth while I wiped away dust and emptied a binful of magazines out of the back — and looking through the glovebox at relics such as old tax discs, receipts for services and tyres and a box of matches. There is also a ring pull from a very old can of pop in the ashtray and some ash deposits in one of the ashtrays in the back, all of which I've left alone as a nod to a previous chapter for the car.

In my wallet, with the receipt for car magazines I'd bought for my dad at the hospital, is the foil silver top from a packet of cigarettes which I found in that glovebox. I'll admit it seems a strange choice when cigarettes undoubtedly played their part in me losing my dad, but it's something very small and insignificant of his I carry with me to give me some sort of comfort.

But it took a while for work to get properly going on the Magnette, mainly due to budget constraints and the fact I didn't know what I was doing. I needed to research where I could get help for things friends wouldn't be able to help me with, such as welding, but I did have a target date in mind. As this was my parents' wedding car, I very much wanted it to serve the same purpose for us when I eventually proposed to Sophie, and this took ages.

I had it in my head I wanted to do it properly, and I wouldn't ask without asking her dad first. One problem was that he lived in Oakham, 120 miles away from us in Billinge, and when I saw him it was always with Sophie, so getting him alone presented my first challenge, until we went to stay with him in the Lake District on the night the EU Referendum result came in.

We spent the day walking and after stopping at a pub, Sophie's dad announced he was going to get the car and instructed the rest of us to stay put to finish our drinks. Despite having two-thirds of an Old Rosie cider left I said I'd go with him to keep him company, which everyone found strange as the only reason I would normally leave two-thirds of a glass of anything would be if I were in immediate mortal danger, but I insisted and we trudged off up a hill together. Straight away my nerves started to betray me as we made mundane conversation in between breaths as we leaned into the slope on our way up. I'd occasionally bang bits of mud off my walking boots with heavy steps as I looked for the right moment, and when I did muster the courage to ask for his attention, I blew it again.

'Chris...'

'Yes, Tom...'

'There are loads of chickens behind that fence, look, loads of them.'

At this point, Chris looked a little perplexed as we were walking past a farm, a place you'd expect to find chickens behind a fence, and a place where you'd expect a 28-year-old to know, through life experience, that one is likely to find them too.

And that was how the conversation went until we got back to Chris's Jaguar and the many moments I could have asked him were gone. I couldn't help but think my next chance was months away.

It actually only took a few hours though — after we'd all gone for a swim. I'd decided against asking him in the changing rooms, a place where Sophie definitely wouldn't walk in on us, because one: We were both in various states of getting undressed. And two: We would both then have to spend the duration of the swim keeping quiet about what we'd just talked about and maybe Sophie would figure something was up. So I waited. And I waited again as we got changed after the swim, not wanting to ask a question of anyone who was putting trousers on anything that may result in a handshake, or worse. What if he was dreading this moment and thought I was terrible for his daughter and he'd have to tell me all of this with one leg in his jeans while I was spraying deodorant. No. I wasn't going to ask here, then.

The walk back to the flat was short and Sophie wasn't waiting as we stepped outside. She was either already on her way back or still getting ready. Right then, this was my last chance.

We started walking back and again my nervousness started rising up through my throat as I squinted because of the sunlight piercing the gaps in the leaves on my right.

'Chris... I need to ask you a question.'

'Yes Tom,' he said with a smile, as if he knew this was coming after the walk to the car.

'I'd like to ask Sophie to marry me, but I wanted to ask you first.'

This sentence was delivered in a series of mumbles and barely escaped my mouth, but his response was fantastic.

'We'll, you can ask her but I can't promise you she'll say "yes".'

I mean, it was true, he couldn't. But by this point Sophie and I had talked about it a little over the course of the past few years. I'd a feeling she would want me to propose in the near-ish future, but for now at least I had her father's permission and that was a huge weight off my mind as we sat down for tea with the only topic of conversation being the pending election results.

Now all I had to do was propose. I'd done my research into what sort of ring Sophie might like and tried to size her finger without her knowing by borrowing a size chart from my mum and holding it to said digit while she slept (more on the results of that test later). Without much fuss, I'd also had the ring made, delivered and hidden in the bottom of my wardrobe for the big event. But with my track record I didn't have anything to worry about for a while... so back to the car.

The key was to make progress — any progress — on the restoration and not think about the project as a whole. I think that's why a lot of restorations end up on bricks and covered up until they either rot or get trailered away after being sold for a fraction of what has been spent on them. This isn't the only reason this happens and it is by no means a criticism. I'm familiar with life getting in the way and the thought of that and selling Maggie was to cross my mind more than once before the end of this tale.

The bodywork could wait for now. I already knew it would be the most expensive part and I already knew it was definitely the bit of the job I was least likely to learn how to do, so having a look to see if the car would turn over would be job number one.

I remembered from the last time my dad tried to start the car that it did turn over. He'd bought a battery from Costco, stuck it on and pressed the starter button to see what would happen. That's when we decided there was an issue with the fuel pump and that's when my head was turned by the bass guitar before we bought one.

I wasn't going to stick a battery on and press the button this time, though, because of what I could see under the bonnet.

Getting under the bonnet was a job in itself. There is a pulley in the passenger footwell, and, predictably, nothing happened when I tried to pull it, with both hands and my feet pressing against the footwell for leverage. I tried wrapping my raw hands in a towel for extra grip — nothing. Having been undisturbed for years, like a lot of things on this car, it was stuck fast. Luckily, while I was swearing and swinging off the pulley, my sister was at my mum's and she had an idea.

'Why don't I help it by lifting the bonnet while you pull?'

Sticking her fingers in-between the slats on the grille, she could find just enough purchase to lift while I rattled the pulley from inside the car (I'd moved on to a rattling technique after ages of unsuccessful pulling as this seemed to move the lever).

It literally took about 30 seconds and then it popped open, no doubt with a force that would have caused the car to shed more rust from its floorpan.

When reading about welding equipment, electronics, all the mechanical parts I would need which would be worn out, I didn't consider the first two jobs would be so rewarding, just clearing a space around the car and finally gaining access to the engine, but then again I was an absolute beginner, so I filed this as a triumph.

The engine was exactly as I remembered it. Fascinating but looking tired, with dirt and calcified remains of what should have been rubber pipes. The washer bottle is the original glass one, with a primitive system of tubes feeding the washers near the windscreen. They work by vacuum, meaning they'll only operate when the car is moving, so if you need to wash your windscreen and the car is stopped, you have to lean out with a cloth. The plug leads, with their red caps displaying 'CHAMPION' were all there, and the manifold under the carburettors with a proud MG logo embossed on the side.

But there was an immediate problem that meant I would not be turning the car over on the button. Every single electrical wire I could see looked fried. Brittle cables, or what was left of them, all led to melted sections which had obviously become too hot at some point. If was going to put a battery on this I could well be lighting a fuse and saying goodbye to the car behind a curtain of flames.

It is possible to turn a car over by hand, but it's easier if you have a starting handle and a place to lock it onto the flywheel, an advantage of the ZA's place in history when a few cars still had these as a safety net if you can't get the car started on the button. So with the help of one of my dad's friends, a man called Pete Brierley who he knew from his days in the Southport branch of the MG Owners' Club in the 1980s, we set about trying to turn it over, which could, in theory, save the cost of an expensive engine rebuild, or even a replacement unit if it would be uneconomical to do.

After the fiasco with getting the bonnet open, you can imagine that this little plan didn't go well. Having locked the starting handle in place, I tried to turn it over. Nothing. Having decided it was because my upper body strength is embarrassingly poor, I asked Pete if he'd try. Nothing.

So we tried together. Nothing.

This prompted us to try with our feet. We also tried hitting the starting handle with a mallet (with a woodblock in-between) starting lightly before moving to full-on pelting it — to the point where the lock on the starting handle snapped off. I ended-up fixing that by putting a screwdriver in the hole which makes a cross section and sawing it off to make a new one.

Right then, plan B.

Plan B was, after some online reading, the diesel method. The idea is that because of diesel's oily properties, a little dribble down each spark plug hole can unstick a seized engine. You basically pour it in, leave it for a few days, and then try to turn the engine over again. Pete would be next available in a couple of weeks, so after nipping to the petrol station with a little can for a fiver's worth of diesel, I carefully put just a little bit in each of the four plug holes.

This being me though, of course, I couldn't wait the full two weeks for Pete's help. Day after day I would go to my mum's and give the mended starting handle a little kick, and each time I would get the same stubborn response. So I did something stupid and poured a bit more diesel in, and then a bit more. I figured it would drain off when we opened the plug on the oil sump.

When Pete next came round, we commenced with our hammering (or is it malleting) and made no progress until, after a particularly enthusiastic wallop, we heard a short and very quiet hiss. It was like when archaeologists find a fragile treasure catching its first glimpse of daylight in 1,000 years after weeks of digging. Everything stopped so we could take a closer look with a gentler tack.

A firm but gentle push saw the starting handle move slightly, and then some more. It was a thorough arm workout, but this engine was turning over for the first time since my dad last pressed the button. I was made-up. (In the end it turned—out that we needn't have bothered, more later).

Next job? Make this thing a rolling chassis.

A theme was developing as, even with the car in neutral, it was impossible to push. Pete showed me where was best to jack the car up, given the precarious state of the metal underneath so we could inspect the wheels — in neutral they should turn quite easily by hand.

A few weeks before, I had looked-up the jacking points in the manual and had a go at raising one side off the ground, just so I could have a nosey underneath. As soon as the jack made contact with the car I wished it hadn't as it just went through the 'metal'

— more like what remained of it — and left a powdery snuff-like mound of rust on the floor. This should have been a red flag, but I was naïve as well as having enough sentimental attachment to the project to put it to the back of my mind.

My last experience had made me very nervous as Pete placed the jack towards the back axle, explaining how at this time it would be one of the strongest points of the car. I didn't breathe as he pushed the lever up and down. He'd asked if I wanted to do it, but I was too nervous. Apart from some creaks and groans — I'm sure I'd creak and groan if I hadn't moved for more than 30 years — the back driver's side wheel was off the ground.

I knew one of the wheels, whether this or one of the other three, or any combination of these, would be stuck because when my dad connected a battery the brake lights came on and stayed there, and sure enough once the car was jacked up we couldn't shift the back wheels.

Pete showed me how to take off the brake drum and try to adjust them so the car would be free to roll. It didn't matter at this point if the brakes weren't working, we weren't going to be driving anywhere, but it needed to be able to be pushed out of the garage for whenever it would inevitably go to a specialist for some work. I just hoped when that day came it would be able to be driven back in again under its own steam, as there was no way anyone would be able to push this car up the steep incline that is my mum's drive.

I suspect a fair few people who have had to change a tyre will have tried to take the wheel nuts off with the car jacked-up, learning by experience that the wheel will turn and make it impossible to loosen them, and then they realise and put the car down, take the wheel nuts off and then remove the wheel. I only know because I've heard about other people doing it, though I'm sure I would have done the same had it happened to me when I was younger. In this instance, I wanted to do the opposite though, in the hope that by doing what I wasn't supposed to, the wheel would free when I started loosening the nut, saving me a job until I asked a mechanic to look at the brakes.

While there are jobs I am happy to have a go at on my car, there are certain ones, even with more experience, I won't tackle. Brakes is one such job. I reckon that unless you are a sublimely confident home mechanic you should leave anything to do with safety, such as your car being able to stop, to a professional.

A day of hammering (or malleting) brake drums off an old car, hands caked in God-knows-what carcinogenic substances, was showing me that this project was becoming increasingly rewarding.

My mum's garage floor was littered with mugs, cold to the touch with varying levels of forgotten brews, and there were a few plates, smudged with oily thumbprints. There was also an whiff of triumph in the air — helped by the fact we'd swapped mine and my mum's Midgets around, so we could use the flat garage floor to change the oil and filters on my car. I'd even fashioned a tool out of a pair of pliers and a screwdriver handle to get my old oil filter off when it wouldn't budge. For extra petrolhead points I wiped my hands on my jeans and planned to nip to the shop on the way home so people would see that I knew how to work on my cars. I didn't think about how I'd ruined a pair of jeans and would make my bathroom smell like a garage when I showered, but I still glowed with the kind of pride my eight-year-old self did when I presented my dad with an Airfix Jaguar E-Type (about the size of the palm of his hand) which I had glued together and painted myself.

Ok, I'd only done some small things that the most basic have-a-go mechanic could do with a cup of tea and YouTube (and I did some things in very much the wrong way) but finally, finally, the car wasn't just sitting there.

I hadn't a clue what should be next on my list after my very small start on getting Maggie back on the road, and took my time deciding what to do.

The Fiat 500 came along after we finally killed the Punto. It had a dent in the driver's side front wing after I'd had a disagreement with a post at a car park and a piece of rear plastic bumper missing from the other side where Sophie had experienced similar.

There had been a period where if you put the steering lock on, it wouldn't start, so you had to put the car in gear, walk behind it and rock it until it clicked, then it would start. It's easy to simply say, well don't pull the steering wheel to lock it, but when that has been the habit of a lifetime it isn't easy to break.

Then there was the huge scrape down the driver's side, going from the driver's door all the way back past the back seat window.

I had scraped it against a concrete pillar outside our cottage. The drive went onto a main road and was difficult to reverse into, especially if the butcher was busy, but I always insisted on reversing into the drive because you shouldn't reverse out onto a main road, and anyone who has tried when it's busy will be able to tell you that you either sit there for what feels like hours, until someone flashes you out, or you don't see someone coming and you annoy them, sometimes having to deal with them tailgating you and gesticulating with every glance you make in your rear view mirror.

And we were both good at parking in this way because we'd had loads of practice.

Until I got complacent and misjudged where the post was. There are scrapes and there are nasty scrapes, and this one was so big it wasn't worth getting fixed as it would cost more than the car was worth.

So what did I do?

I tried to fix it myself.

I like trips to Halfords, and even if I've only gone in for a can of WD40 I will walk around and survey the tools and car cleaning products, so I decided I would peruse their spray paint aisle and fettle the scrape I'd made down the side of Sophie's car.

Now then.

If you are ever thinking of doing a home paint job like this, don't.

Painting a car is a very precise skill and as well as someone with that skill, a successful repair also requires a precise set of conditions to make sure it looks good and dries properly. And you also absolutely must have the right paint colour.

You can find the right paint by matching the code of your car's colour code, usually found under the bonnet on a vehicle information sticker with the matching number in the little book on the end of the shelf in Halfords. It's easier with old cars because, for example, MG had specific names for a handful of colours and you just knew that you needed Harvest Gold, or Vermillion, or Damask Red. Nowadays, suppliers make pretty good matches of these colours and you're good to go. The problem you have with classics is if they have been resprayed in a slightly off shade and you go with what you think is the right one. That's why you need the professionals.

With this knowledge, I assumed that by knowing the Punto was from 2007 and was blue I'd be good to go. I wasn't going to attempt to fix the dent because the kits for doing that looked as if they were destined to fail, but at least I could cover the scratches and huge scuff, about a quarter of a door's worth, and impress Sophie. She was on a hen night in Blackpool and I thought it would be the perfect chance to get the job done.

Halfords, however, listed a handful of shades for a 2007 Fiat Punto, and in the book they all looked similar.

So what did I do?

Wait?

Get the right code?

Save my money and leave it?

I bought the colour I thought it was based on what was in the book. I know what you're thinking and I know the second word is 'hell'.

While Sophie was drinking cocktails from willy straws with

her hen party mates, I laid out my can of primer, top coat and paint on the drive at home, reading the instructions to sand down and smooth the scratches before putting on a base coat that would take hours to dry. I was a bit unsure of myself, but thought 'what the heck' and started sanding the side of the car. It looked even worse with every swish of my hand.

I knew it wasn't going well but had gone too far so, with an even more coarse surface than I began with, I decided it wasn't going to get any better and started to spray the grey primer on the side of the car – only I was in the great outdoors in the midst of the kind of wind you only notice in the air when you are spray-painting something. Little flecks of grey began to appear in places I really didn't want them to... such as windows and door handles. I stopped and left it to dry, this job that really should have been done with the car inside a garage.

A couple of hours later, that same sky began to spit infrequent drops of rain, so I went out to the car and touched the primer. It wasn't totally wet, not coming off on my fingertips certainly, but it definitely felt sticky. I looked up and the clouds glowered down, looking threatening. 'Fuck it,' I thought and got to work with the blue, though daylight was also fading by now.

The feeling of wishing I hadn't started began to feel heavy in my stomach. Even in semi-darkness I could see the colours didn't match. Then the rain really came, pockmarking and streaking my afternoon's work.

The good news is that it was fully dark when the time came to drive to Blackpool and pick Sophie up. She was in too good a mood to care about paint (although hadn't seen my efforts at this point). I made sure to get up early the next morning to survey the damage and come up with a plan.

You can imagine the image I was greeted with on the gravelled drive, a couple of hours before the whole village would see my handiwork as they blocked the car in, one by one, queueing for their sausages and joints for roasting.

I spent a good hour scraping the paint off with hot water and a credit card, destined to find little flecks of blue paint in my trouser pockets and wallet for months after.

This mishap, coupled with a spongey oil sump that would surely crack and empty itself the next time we hit a pothole, spelled the end of Edith, but there were more pressing car concerns on my mind as Sophie then chose the 500 as the car she would thereafter burden with getting us both to work.

15

The Appraisal

2012 BMW 1 Series
A car I loved driving, even though it was the poor man's choice when it came to BMWs. But this was ours, so of course there were problems, and an unhappy sales experience ruined this car for me before we'd even left the forecourt.

'It's not an estimate, but from what we can see you're looking at seven to ten grand. Obviously, this will probably change because when we start we'll uncover more that needs doing.'

So seven to ten grand was a minimum. It would probably be nearer double that, I thought. Restoration projects rarely come in anywhere near their budget. My initial reaction was 'dream shattered, then.'

I'd been researching specialists to take on the bulk of getting Maggie at least solid and running, and with that comes fear that you'll have your car trailered to a garage many miles away and end up running out of money with no way to get it back. Luckily for me, Quest Classic Car Restoration was three miles away. I knew, for this reason above many others, that if a specialist was going to help me I wanted it to be them.

There was a slight fly in the ointment in that I didn't have seven to ten grand, or anything close for that matter, but what I did have was a plan. I knew I could save a little each month — maybe a little under £200 if I played hardball and didn't spend silly amounts of money each month on lattes with whichever flavoured sugar syrup was in vogue, and if I was honest with Quest, we could put in place a payment plan. I was initially cautious of this as I'd read stories of restoration companies keeping hold of people's cars when payment was disputed and stripped-down cars were rescued on the back of trailers by desperate owners driving hundreds of miles with brown envelopes loaded with hastily scraped together wads of cash. I got the impression I was an unusual customer. Instead of spending six figures on an investment opportunity, never to be driven more than the distance from a trailer to a parking space at a coveted show to collect prizes for their rich owner, I was spending money I shouldn't really be thinking about throwing at a car (that actually isn't worth very much) because of a sentimental attachment.

It was basically the start of a grief project (and one that would give me further grief). My options were to have the car brought home to be put back in the same spot it had spent the last 30 years without having to pay anything for the appraisal, or go ahead with a plan. I decided to be honest. I could beg, borrow and save maybe £2,000 with enough notice, so we'd go in instalments of the same. I asked them to keep track of everything, and when they got to £2,000 stop work and ring me. I'd pay-up and decide whether to ask them to carry on, or have a break. They agreed and I was shocked. It was the answer I wanted, so proper work could finally begin on the car, but there was also a very small part of me hoping this wouldn't be agreeable so that I could say the decision was taken out of my hands and I could move on, though deep down I knew that was never an option.

It had been a few days since Maggie had moved for the second time in my lifetime. I'm glad Pete and I unstuck the brakes because shortly after, my mum replaced her garage door and the fitter said the garage needed to be empty. Not a problem as far as the Midget was concerned because this could simply be driven out, and even if it couldn't, anyone who has ever pushed a Midget, which I'm guessing is most people who have owned one, will know that this isn't the most physically demanding task.

The Magnette was another matter. By modern standards it is a small car, but it weighs an absolute ton, well nearly bang on a ton at 1,090kg compared with the 735kg Midget. There was also the problem of my mum's steep drive. It would only nearly be an exaggeration to say it's on a 45-degree angle, so once Maggie was out of the garage, how on earth were we going to get it back?

With the garage door people on their way, we'd have to deal with that later. Right now I was faced with the prospect of pushing a car with no brakes off what was basically a ramp and hoping the steering was up to scratch.

I inflated the tyres, put the car in neutral and took a deep breath. I could roll the car by putting my shoulder through the open driver's window, giving me my left arm to steer, but as soon as the wheel touched the top of the drive, it was clear this thing was going to run away with me and straight into the car parked on the neighbour's drive across the road, which would have been a nightmare. I didn't have time to think about this, though, as I flung myself half through the window to try to put the moving wrecking ball into gear, which would hopefully have stopped it on the hill, and I was lucky — it did. No one's car was damaged, only a slight pain running throughout my left hand side, though I am told my pain threshold is shockingly low, especially for a person who loved to play rugby when growing up.

We still had a problem in that the car was in what was going to be the path of people carrying a garage door, it still needed to move. With the feeling of a little boy wanting to retrieve a football sent over the garden fence (a feeling I was familiar with as a child) I rang the neighbours' doorbell to explain why I wanted them to move their car off their own drive.

'No, I don't want to leave my car on your drive. I would like you to move it just in case my car, which doesn't run and has no brakes, decides to not let me steer it safely past your lovely, fairly new vehicle.'

Path cleared, I jumped in the Magnette, about to steer a moving ZA for the first time, though not under circumstances I imagined. Despite being used to the steering on a classic car, this was a different beast to the Midget entirely, and there wasn't enough time between taking the car out of gear and being confronted with the neighbours' hedge to heave the huge steering wheel around enough times, and I resorted to slamming it back into gear to stop it just before said hedge was given a new, car-width-sized entranceway. At least I was now on flat ground, and with many minutes of pushing, shoving and adjusting the steering, I was able to get Maggie to the side of the road before any garage doors could be removed and whacked into it, and it also gave me a chance to survey the car both in 360 degrees and in daylight for the very first time.

I was struck by how small it looked in the context of being near other cars, and just how battered some of the bodywork is, though even then I had decided that if any scars weren't in need of repair to make it safe, I would leave them as they were. Each dent and scuff is a story, even if no one is around to recount the tale, and I always knew I wanted this part of the car to be on show.

Despite these lovely few moments, which included taking a few photos, giving the car a quick polish and opening doors which had been constricted by the garage wall, I was well aware we had a very big problem on our hands. Despite my mum living on the quietest of quiet residential streets, it could not stay where it was. We were, somehow, going to have to try to get it back up the slope and into the garage.

My sister's husband, Heapy — the drummer in the band we'd supported Bon Jovi with — was my first port of call, along with our mutual friend Rob, a fellow car nut who can shift a heavy object or two. Heapy called his photographer friend Gaz, who can also hold up a rugby union scrum on his own. My sister would steer and my older brother James would provide additional support at the back. The additional weight provided by having my sister in the driving seat would be negligible, and having someone to steer in the car would allow us to carry out our mission with enough speed to get us up the slope. Luckily, everyone was available and within half an hour we were poised, in the middle of the road, for our first run.

Our battle plan was to go together and use speed — attack being the best form of defence. A car of just over a ton up a slope at a near-45-degree angle wasn't going to be easy. Some reading this may disagree, but for us it was a big ask. It's about the same as a big rugby union pack weight — and don't tell me there was no push back, the slope, remember.

Not going as far as 'bind, set, engage,' we did decide we'd all go together, on three.

'One.'

'Two.'

'Three.'

Immediately after we started pushing, my knackered Converse trainers lost their grip on the tarmac and my place as blindside prop, with my shoulder pressing the headlight, was compromised by the mishap. A scrum would have turned, but the car kept moving — nowhere near the pace we needed. My brother had also gone down by this point, and by the time I caught up my hands were on Rob's back and my input useless. Halfway up the drive we had to dig in and ease the car back down gently. Remember, my sister had no brakes at her disposal.

I decided to remove my shoes and socks. It would hurt, but better stand on stones and get trod on than to slip again. And we decided to start from further down the road in a bid to pick-up more speed.

'One.'

'Two.'

'Three.'

Grunts and rushed breathing, growls and cries let curtain twitchers know of our effort, and as we raced up the drive, my sister steering expertly (and in reverse) to point the car in its place without putting the Midget on our left into danger, we all thought we were going to do it. Then the lip at the top of the drive, where the tarmac met the concrete of the garage floor, made it 2-0 to gravity. Our efforts were spent, and it was harder to bring the car down safely this time, but my sister was on top form and managed to force it into gear halfway down to give us a slower bunny hop down the drive.

We were already knackered, but our progress from halfway up the drive to nearly there had given us some confidence.

A captain's team talk.

'You all need to shout. If you shout as we push it will make us more aggressive and give us an extra ten per cent. We need five percent to get us over that ridge. We're doing it this time.'

I know, give me a job on the coaching staff of any international team. A talk like that could guide the USA rugby league team to victory over the All Blacks at their own game.

'One.'

'Two.'

'Three.'

The people buried in the cemetery a couple of miles down the road stirred as we roared up the road and eased the car up the drive. My shoulder was in just the right place, touching metal under the headlight and I had a nice grip of the grille with my free hand. Someone behind me had locked on tightly and their strength was pushing me forward. It felt effortless as again the car was piloted perfectly into position. Until we hit the bloody ridge again. Everything stopped, but we didn't move. The back wheels were on the ridge, but the car was still bearing down on us at the steep angle. Stalemate.

'Don't stop, lads.'

A voice, I don't know whose, announced an executive decision that we weren't coming back down this drive with a car on our backs.

'Steady yourselves. Brace your legs. If we get the back wheel over, the rest will go in, no problem.'

By this point my mum had come out to check our progress, and make sure she wouldn't be responsible for blocking the road for much longer.

I could just about muster a word or two while having my neck crushed by my car.

'How close is the back wheel to the garage, mum?'

'It's on the lip of the concrete, love.'

One more push.

It was with more of a whimper than the triumphant battle cry of a few minutes before, but you could tell when the back wheels had successfully found their way into the garage because of a collective groan. And like we'd hoped, the rest of the car slotted in no problem.

'Put it in gear and get some bricks!'

My mum's instructions signalled her desperation for this car not to roll back down the drive, and we obliged, quickly.

It was late afternoon and probably too late for drinking caffeine to be a good idea, but it was one of the best coffees I've ever had. You can go to the ends of the earth looking for the best speciality coffee (and I sort of have) and I am a coffee snob, I run on the stuff, but give me a mug of instant made by my mum any day. I don't know what it is, but it doesn't matter which jar it has come from, it's the best brew in the world, every time.

The ZA in Penkridge in May 1972, above, just before the Gosling family sold it

Above: Will's 1976 Midget, NTB 300R, and Tom's mum and dad's wedding day in March, 1983. Below: The couple with their MGs, including Maggie, in the early 1980s.

The author's parents enjoying some Manchester sunshine in 1982.

Tom, aged five, testing out the 'wayback' seats in the Montego with his brother.

Enlisting a group of friends to push the Magnette back up the steep drive at Tom's mum's house, left, before its restoration.

The Wigan Evening Post's coverage of Tom's band's 15 minutes of fame, right.

Below: The Magnette leaves home for the first time in 33 years, as it heads to Quest Classic Vehicle Restoration.

The size of the task became even more apparent as rotten metal was cut (or more accurately fell) away, left.

Zen and the Art of Motor Car Maintenance – fixing the brakelight switch on the MG Midget, right. Working on these vehicles requires all sorts of yoga postures and inward exploration.

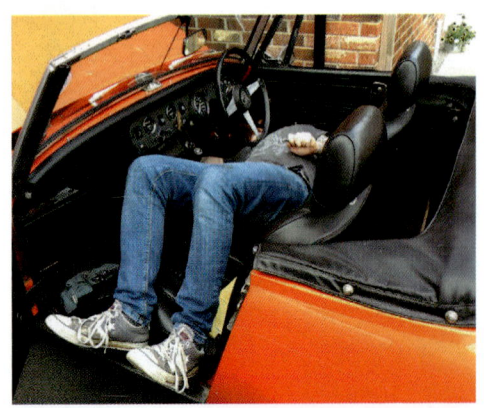

Seeing the ZA in such a state, below, as old metal was ripped away, felt like a real low point.

New sills are put into place as the Magnette's body work goes under major surgery, above.

A freshly-painted rebuilt engine awaits being reunited with the car, above left. One of JED's jobs has been to take Tom's brother Joe to his school leaving dinner, above right. Tom's sister's Morris Minor, right, leaves her house for the last time after being sold.

Left: Otis the Labrador helps Gary Brunskill refit the back seat in 2019.

Right: Putting the interior back in the ZA, 2019

Above: No bonnet – the very first time Tom ever heard the Magnette spring to life.

Right: Tom's first drive in the ZA lasted fewer than four miles before it ground to a halt.

Top: Home safely in the second drive of Maggie, after the false start. Right: Gary Brunskill takes a look after a breakdown.

Left: Gary Brunskill and Bill Parr have worked hard to get Maggie running smoothly. Below left: Out and about, summer 2023. Below right: How many MG buffs does it take to change a lightbulb?

Tom and Maggie go out for a drive soon after the ZA was put back on the road

It's friends like that which put things like this into perspective. Ok, it wasn't a car-related favour per-se, but nobody except me had anything to gain from the help of those five people, yet they dropped what they were doing to come and help me out. It made me think people will be there when things go wrong further down the line, and maybe this crazy project was worth pursuing after all, just not for a bit after this episode.

In the meantime, many months after asking her dad, I finally got the chance to ask Sophie if she fancied putting a label on the ride we were on.

We were never official, we'd never been on a date before moving in together, we'd never said 'my girlfriend/boyfriend.'

I'd had the ring for ages, tucked away in the bottom of my wardrobe, waiting for its big reveal, but there was no plan because there couldn't be. I couldn't propose in a setting like a restaurant because that would mortify the pair of us and the only place I really wanted to do it came with a very specific set of circumstances which could absolutely not be manipulated.

Sophie had thought I was going to propose on a trip to Edinburgh we'd treated ourselves to in the December after I'd asked her dad in the June. I'd been decadent and booked a very swanky room and an equally swanky meal, and I'll admit it had crossed my mind to ask her in our favourite city. I'd billed the trip as a late birthday treat to myself, but in the end the ring never made it out of the house, because at the last minute I decided that bringing it would put pressure on me to ask the question, even if the moment wasn't quite right, and I would be nervous throughout the trip. Better for both of us if I waited. But I didn't expect the wait to be another five months, almost a year after I'd asked her dad.

But this particular night in May, 2017 was spot on. We'd been up putting the world to rights and listening to records until it was starting to get light outside. They are the kind of nights we probably won't get now until the kids are older and you can't decide you're going to stay up all night and chat — they have to just happen. Then as dawn was breaking, Sophie had an idea.

'Do you want to go up the Lump and watch the sun come up.'

Bingo.

That same hill where we went for our walk when she first met my dad, the same hill where I would watch the sun come up when I was at college, the same hill my mum took us to fly a kite when we were kids. It meant a lot to me that The Lump had come to mean a lot to Sophie, too, and I decided this would be a nice way to make it special for both of us in a new way. I quickly shoved a couple of bottles of cola in a backpack, some mugs and what was left of the rum. Then I ran upstairs to get what I hoped would become Sophie's new engagement ring.

I do tend to faff though. I take longer than Sophie to get ready to go out, and whether I'm making a brew or changing a child out of a dirty top, I never miss an opportunity to faff. I tidy as I go in the kitchen, and I've been known to reorganise cupboards while the various components of a cake await mixing, and a simple nappy change becomes a game lasting half an hour. If I need to put shoes on to accompany you somewhere, better give me plenty of notice, I might walk past a picture that needs straightening or a bit of skirting board that needs a crack filling, sanding and painting. I can't help it.

'Just got to nip upstairs,' I said, with my coat on so I could hide the ring in my pocket. 'Won't be long.'

Sophie has since told me she wondered why she could hear the sliding door on the wardrobe clang if I already had my coat on. Then once I had the box in my hand I had to check the ring was still there, then I had to take it out the box, so I could put it back in the box to make sure it was really there.

And then I had to put the box in my pocket, taking it out again to check the ring hadn't vanished in the five seconds between me last seeing it and now. I was ready.

I tried not to be awkward or quiet on the walk through the

woods, gradually revealing more of the trees in the distance as the light of the sun below the horizon started to peer through the gaps. I had the idea that I would wait for the perfect song before asking, but in reality I was so nervous I waited and waited until the rum, and the phone battery, had gone. I wasn't missing my chance though.

'Are you being serious?'

I mean, her dad was right — he couldn't promise she would say 'yes.'

I thought I was being about as serious as I could be, I was on one knee and I had my hand in my pocket, ready for the big reveal of the ring I had hidden away for so many months. I took it and opened the box.

This showed I was, indeed, serious, and while Sophie loved the ring, it was obvious very early on that my size chart mission had failed as it was far too big — a resize on the cards then — but she was very happy, then he expression changed a few seconds later and she asked: 'Why are you still on one knee?'

'Because you haven't said "yes" yet.'

We decided early on though that we weren't going to launch into wedding planning mode immediately. We would get married when the time was right for us, and enjoy the process, rather than set a date and the stress until the day. I also had a car I wanted to fix. If Maggie could do the same job for me as it did for my mum and dad, I'd be a very happy bloke.

This was Friday 19th May, well Saturday 20th by the time we'd watched the sun come up, had bacon sandwiches, called my older brother who was on holiday in the States and invited my family over for champagne that evening, which I would put on my credit card and hope the weight of car expenses would hide it when it came to statement time.

We'd hardly recovered from celebrating when, once again on a *Wigan Observer* deadline morning, my phone sent a shudder through my spine.

News of a death in the family was brought by a call on the landline in the middle of the night when I was a kid. No one has landlines anymore, and calls bringing such feared news in the small hours are missed because phones are on silent and people sleep through them. These days you find out via WhatsApp. Unless you're me, and then summons to get to the hospital quickly, or that someone has died, comes on *Obby* deadline.

On the night Sophie and I got engaged, I had a missed call from my grandad — my mum's dad. He was 97 years old, had only recently stopped driving and was shot at by Nazis on D-Day.

He was 19 when the Second World War started and was involved throughout in the 253rd West Lancashire Field Company — the Royal Engineers. I'd called him earlier in the day for a chat, and we'd talk about everything from life to rugby, and with him being from St Helens, he was a seasoned supporter of the town's rugby league team, the most bitter rivals of my beloved Wigan.

He left a voicemail: 'Sorry I missed your call, I didn't hear it in the hall. I was cooking a piece of fish. I'll speak to you soon.' I'd call him back when I wasn't drunk. I didn't call him all weekend, and on the Tuesday morning my mum had phoned me to say she couldn't get an answer. I told her to wait until lunchtime and I'd go with her, when the *Obby* had gone to press. It would be fine, I thought, he will have accidentally unplugged his phone from the wall.

She didn't take my advice, and halfway through the morning she called to say he was dead in his chair.

It must have been awful for my mum to have gone to her dad's house, on her own, and find him like that, and I don't think until writing it down I've ever really thought about how that would feel. I had my mum sitting opposite when it happened to me, and I was expecting it to happen. To be on your own and for it to be a shock must have been awful, and very long wait for the cavalry of my siblings and cousins to arrive while she was there. I still have the phone with that voicemail on it (but no charger) and still have the numbers of both grandparents and my dad stored in my contacts. One comfort, though, is how my grandad went. There were no hospital visits, no tubes, catheters... parking meters. He'd simply been to town with one of my cousins, come home, sat in his chair and not got up, after an amazing 97-year life. That'll do.

While we were waiting for the funeral directors, the edge was taken off the shock and the upset by the visit of the priest. My mum's sister decided we ought to call him, you know, let's make sure everything is present and correct in the queue to get into heaven and all that, and what followed was a very awkward, and very long prayer with the family standing in a circle, around my dead grandad in his chair, and I found it really difficult to stifle a laugh when someone's phone rang at an appropriately solemn part of the proceedings.

The following month, with my grandad's eulogy confidently delivered and folded into the pocket of a blazer and hung in the wardrobe, my dad's dad ended-up in Whiston Hospital.

Approaching his 90th birthday in June, 2017, my dad's dad, Jim, was one of those people who knew everybody and could do anything. Having left school at 13 to go to work and help look after his family because of his own dad's health, he ran his own business fitting out shops and helping people with construction projects on their homes before teaching joinery at Wigan Technical College, which is now Wigan and Leigh College.

He built his own house in the '50s and it was full of ingenious ideas. One was the landing wall, which had a hinge and you could pull it down to make a platform and block off the stairs for cleaning the window, though I used it as a road to play with my dad's old toy cars. Anything you needed making he could do, from balconies and conservatory frames to rabbit hutches and guitar pedal boards. I spent a lot of time in his garage when I was small hammering nails into bits of wood, unaccompanied on a few occasions. He even cut car wheels out of a broom on his circular saw for me (the one thing in the garage I wasn't allowed to touch) so I could hammer them onto blocks of wood to make my own cars.

Jim had two sons and a wife, and out-lived them all (my uncle died of liver cancer in 1998 and my grandma, known simply as 'Ma' died in 2005) and when my dad died he stayed in more, so we visited often and my mum did all his shopping for him.

When my mum's dad died, Jim's health declined rapidly, to the point where he wasn't eating the meals we prepared for him and we were having to help him to bed each day. Deciding to take him to hospital wasn't easy, and after a night in A&E, he was admitted to a ward, not changing our routine much other than our daily drives were an extra few minutes towards Liverpool instead of St Helens. He peaked and troughed for a bit until he stopped having his good days, and in August he moved to a care home in Rainford, near St Helens. We continued to bring his papers and Lucozade long after he'd stopped asking for them, and we knew it was really time to worry when we were the only ones using them. He lasted six more days.

The summer had shaken the family dynamic, leaving my mum as head of the roost and us finding our geographical circle shrink to within the boundaries of Billinge. While she had been holding everyone together for years, knowing there was no one 'above' her was a big change to deal with, it's a crutch I take for granted. Whatever happens, my mum is there for advice, reassurance, the first line of defence. For that to be gone for her must have been scary, but we all tried to support her as best we could and try to find other things to concentrate on. For me, that wasn't a problem. Wedding planning and cars should be enough.

In September, the Magnette had been loaded onto the back of a flatbed and carted a couple of miles down the road to Quest for an assessment and, hopefully, for work to be carried out. This was also the month our two became a three — we bought a Labrador puppy and called him Otis.

It was a couple of days after I got the devastating seven to ten grand phone call.

Of all the decisions in life I have made with my heart and not my head, and there are many, this is the one that I knew at the time made the least sense — but having organised the billing every £2,000 and taking stock approach, I decided bringing the car back home again, untouched, was too much to bear.

In the meantime, Sophie's Fiat 500 was causing us problems. The clutch kept slipping, causing the revs to climb when the car was in gear and after visiting friends in Manchester one evening, it let us down in a big way where the M602 meets the M62, not a million miles from where Salford rugby league club play at the AJ Bell Stadium. The temperature warning light came on and told me to stop the car and standing on the side of the motorway, in the dark, made us both fall out with it. It turned out the problem was that one of the plastic pipes in the cooling system had split, shedding coolant.

Our recovery driver asked: 'How far are you from home?'

On hearing it was at least 20 miles, he agreed we couldn't risk it, and to be fair he arrived quickly and got us home in one piece, though even after getting the problem fettled, it was time for the Fiat to go.

With long distance driving to see Sophie's family becoming more common, we decided to see what was out there. We'd already been tentatively looking at prices of BMW's compact 1 Series online.

We'd found one at a dealership not too far from where we lived, and booked a test drive thinking nothing of it.

What followed was one of the worst shopping experiences of my life.

After pulling into the forecourt and being greeted by the usually friendly-at-first salesman, we were promptly given the keys to a lovely-looking red 1 Series and told to take our time. Sophie drove for about ten minutes, then we swapped, and I drove it back. I will admit that driving a BMW for the first time is a superb experience, especially given the cars in my repertoire up to that point. Yes, it was only a five-year-old baby BMW and no, it wasn't a classic, but there was a robustness and comfort about it I liked. Yes, we'd think about it.

Only thinking about it wasn't an option.

After we disembarked and I did a walkaround, deciding that I'd ask them to change some tired-looking tyres if we were to buy it, the same gentleman approached.

'Ah, if you don't come back straightaway then we know you like it.'

I thought that was odd, and what followed was more than an hour of the most aggressive sales tactics I'd ever been subjected to. I cringe looking back, and wish I had been more confident in taking the Fiat's keys off the table and going home when I first felt uncomfortable. Instead, I let myself sink deeper and deeper into this awkwardness until the only way out, it seemed, was to take the car just to get it over with. It's one of those evenings in my life I wish I could revisit and tell myself to get a grip, but it was an important lesson learned.

In an earlier life I sold mobile phones, so I know how people behave when they work on commission and I know that sometimes you'll push something on someone when they're not fully on board. But I would always like to think I at least listened.

Taking the keys for the Fiat from across the desk and putting them on top of his file (a shitty move in itself) the salesperson asked what I wanted with regards finance. I showed him the car on the dealer's website and said I'd like to come back tomorrow and pay the price listed on the website and take the car.

'The car went up in price today, the website hasn't updated.'

I'd like to, at this point, have told him in that case I wasn't interested and left.

What I actually did was continue to sit there to look for a more polite way out.

He then went through a finance deal — I can't remember how much it was for — but it was more than I wanted to pay. I knew a bank loan for the same money was a lot cheaper and if we were going to have the car I wanted to get a loan and come back with the cash. My lack of confidence let me take the crap that the car would be gone tomorrow because 'someone had already been in that day', and another had had their credit check on it knocked back. All the tried and tested bullshit tactics that I swallowed because of my lack of confidence.

After 'agreeing' a finance deal, we were then escorted to another office where scratch and damage insurance, a service plan and alloy protection were thrust upon us with the promise of grave consequences if we didn't. By this point it was dark, we hadn't been home after work and I decided I would just get a loan from the bank the next day and call up to cancel all of these agreements. I'd take the hit on my credit rating and stick two fingers up to the bullies' commission. Getting home would be quicker if I just signed the forms than to argue. And for that reason, I regretted the BMW from the night it arrived. When you make a big financial decision, there's always the talk, justifying it to yourselves and each other, but none of that happened on the way home, despite the journey being in a nicer car than the Fiat. (And I didn't argue for new tyres.) It had just become a problem to sort.

Thankfully, the bank gave me a loan without a problem and the money was in my account the following day. I phoned the finance company and settled that, then called the dealer to cancel the add-ons.

'But you wanted them yesterday,' said the bully.

I found my confidence, separated by a few miles from the source of the discomfort.

'Well I only signed-up for them so I could escape. Please cancel them now.'

Where was that the night before?

With newly-tightened finances, while I wasn't exactly dreading the first bill for Maggie, I wasn't looking forward to it either. When taking out the loan to pay for the BMW, I'd added some on to my request to deal with the Magnette, and a week after my 30th birthday, the first bill arrived, with a CD of photographs, a shade over the £2,000 stopping point.

In just over three months they'd spent 52 hours on my car — a slower pace then they normally work owing to the budget constraints I'd set — but it wasn't lost on me that with my current level of car knowledge, their 52 hours' worth of work would have easily taken more than a year, and looking at what was left of the car, I'd have been gutted to wait so long to go, what looked like to me at least, backwards.

This, of course, wasn't the case. In order for much-needed welding work to be done, the original leather interior was carefully removed and now resided, wrapped-up, in my mum's garage, and the engine had also been taken out to be rebuilt. My diesel method of unseizing it had only managed to produce a sticky, oily gunk which meant the engine needed stripping and rebuilding anyway. A compression test had revealed the valves and piston rings needed attention anyway, so I could have saved myself a lot of bother by not trying to be a home mechanic in that instance.

Elsewhere, the exhaust system was removed, including the exhaust pipe which was so corroded you could rub it into a powder between your finger and thumb and scraping away thick layers of underseal which hid a plethora of sins and problems, a sure sign this car was last wide awake in the era of the botch which was the late 1970s and early '80s.

On top of this, welding had already begun with the offside (driver's side) rear inner chassis first to get attention with some panels Quest had fabricated.

The list looked impressive, but all I saw in the pictures were pieces of metal where holes occupied space where car should be. My thoughts were that someone without sentimental attachment would have walked away after inspection of the car. It really was crusted to the point of no return underneath. By no means was it even remotely economical to save it. But here we were. I paid the bill and asked them to crack on.

With Maggie's restoration now in full swing, and approaching the point of no return, at least our daily driver was sorted. The BMW wouldn't let us down.

16

Cap in Hand

2010 Vauxhall Insignia TDI
Simply put, the best car under 35 years old I've ever owned.

It may have been 'the ultimate driving machine' but that slogan is pretty useless when only weeks after buying the BMW an error message intermittently started displaying on the dash. 'Drivetrain error: Continue journey at a moderate speed, full performance not available, have the problem checked by Service.'

One of the add-ons the dealer had sold to us, which I kept, was a service plan which included parts. We'd had the car for a matter of weeks, so I figured whatever it was wouldn't be blamed on us.

Wrong.

A video message popped-up on my phone while the car was being looked at, by the dealer's mechanic. The camera went under the car and panned into a dark spot with absolutely nothing visible.

'As you can see here, the problem is your clutch has worn out. It's £800 to repair.'

A car that needed a new clutch at just over 30,000 miles.

Fantastic. I can't imagine what the previous owner was doing to kill it so quickly. I argued my case only to be told, as you will have guessed, that the clutch is a 'wear and tear item.'

When you consider the fact I'd replaced the tyres, within a few months of owning the BMW, it had cost more than the Fiat would have cost to fix. My mind also jumped back to the problems we had with the Fiat. Were our clutch habits so poor that we were just killing them? I reassessed my driving technique and tried to be as bluntly honest with myself as possible, but after consulting friends, YouTube, driving manuals, I tried to reassure myself these faults with the cars weren't accelerated by my driving. Either way, I'd already had enough of the BMW.

In the meantime, work was progressing on the Magnette quickly, and the £2,000 limit for each bill seemed to have been forgotten about when Quest's latest letter landed on the mat on 12th January, 2018.

I remember the bill sitting on the floor in the hall, it was a Friday and I tended to have them off work in lieu of Sunday subbing shifts where I'd pull the copy together for the following day's sports section and lay it out in the paper. The envelope was too heavy to be a couple of pages and the CD-rom of images that came with the first bill. I filed to the back page with a knot in my stomach.

They'd spent 121 hours on my car, at £35 per hour, and spent another £875 on materials. Then there was VAT on top. I didn't have two grand, never mind £6,384.84. That amounted to a lot of freelance articles.

'That'll mean I can't have a bathroom then.'

That was mum, on the other end of the phone, who I'd called before sitting down. She knew from my voice something was up and even more so when I asked if she was sitting down. She was about to get in the car. I didn't know whether driving as a distraction from the news was a good or a bad thing with what I was about to tell her.

'Just give me a figure.'

Normally, this would again be time for that trait to arise that I share with my mum — i.e. to become emotional and consumed by everyday crises and fly off the handle at little things like an unexpected increase in pet insurance, entirely preoccupied by such problems until they are resolved. However this particular issue was so bad we somehow kept cool. My mum, I'm sure, knows how grateful I am — but I do feel I don't show her that enough.

My pride was also hurt. I needed a bung, and I hate asking for them. And this wasn't just any bung. It was a small property deposit-sized bung at a time when she was planning to refurbish a bathroom so dated it still had a bidet.

On reflection, it was a bloody good job my mum loves that car and even more of a good job that she has to love me by default. I felt spoiled, even more so than a time when I was about nine and we were on a family day out to Southport. We just did the fairground and a walk around the shops after emptying the claw machines of all the plush toys in the arcade. I know they're fixed, but my mum genuinely seems to have a knack for getting the prizes out of them. (We were politely given a binbag to put the toys in and asked to leave by an arcade manager in Blackpool once). Sometimes, on these days out we'd be treated to something bigger like a rugby ball or a CD. On this particular day in Southport we'd gone to Woolworths and I went to look at games for my Sega Saturn console, and I pulled the sufficient faces required to get my dad to agree to buying the Fifa 97 football game for me. He wasn't happy about it, and while I never threw a tantrum in public past toddlerdom, the pulled bottom lip and sulking was — I'd like to think — rare. I should have been happy, but I never felt right about the way I got that game, and I even wanted to change my mind as my dad queued, but I think he knew and used it to teach me an expensive (£29.99) lesson.

Fast-forward 20-odd years and after seeing the transfer go

into my account, and doing nowhere near the appropriate amount of grovelling, I quickly rummaged through the drawers for a card reader that had a battery that would work for long enough for me to transfer the money over to Quest. I thought I'd better phone them to make sure it had landed.

'Mate, you didn't need to pay so quickly. With the amount we figured we'd stop work and we were expecting you to take a while to pay us.'

I really should listen to my own advice much more often. One of the best things I have ever heard is, 'Wait a little bit,' and you can apply it to any situation. Survey the lay of the land. If you're feeling stressed or angry, hold your horses. If you have a big decision or a crisis in front of you, mull it over. If you're having the best day of your life, stand still and take it in for a minute.

This has now translated into 'Woah... woah... woah!', which is what I say to my son when he's about to jump off the arm of the couch or make a beeline for the road while I'm swiping at him to try and catch his hood in my fingers. He started repeating it when he was around 18 months old and I have got it from my dad, who did the same to me. if I were to ever get asked one of those best advice questions by a lifestyle columnist, I'd just say 'Woah.'

The extra time would have been handy, but I would probably have still needed some help. Having said that, seeing the progress on the car, in the form of an itemised bill and in pictures, gave me a hunger (and the stupidity) to ask Quest to carry on, just at a slightly slower pace as I would definitely not be able to find any more than £2,000 next time. I couldn't ask for another bung and I had one more card up my sleeve for the next bill.

A decent chunk of that 121 hours was a full day spent scraping sludge from the engine block and steam cleaning it, which was a further problem having been caused by my trying to free it off with diesel. That had mixed with the decades-old oil to form a substance which would put any YouTuber showing kids how to make slime to shame.

Elsewhere, heavy filler was chipped away — a popular way to cheaply fix rusting cars — and work began on fitting new sills, while panels were fabricated and welded onto areas where rusted metal was cut away.

Once the engine block was cleaned, that was then sprayed, the only part of the car to look anything like in good condition, while I was left to look at my CD Rom of photographs showing me what looked like a shell of something that looked like it might once have been a car. If we stopped now, we'd be in a right mess. The interior was still wrapped and in my mum's garage, the engine was in (very clean and freshly-sprayed) bits and all over the place while the car itself was minus its doors and looking like it would crumble at any moment, save for the shiny new bits of metal sticking out from the rest of what was left. I needed to at least get as much of it put back together as I could before we stopped for a break.

Work had stopped on 9th January, 2018, and Quest resumed on 12th March, with welding to the offside floorpan and rear chassis suspension stop. Basically, they continued welding new metal into where rusted crust had been cut away, what remained to be cleaned of the engine was done before it was rebuilt, and more rusted panels were removed.

In the meantime, without a plan to start paying my mum back, I played the last remaining card up my sleeve to raise funds.

I sold my Midget.

The decision to part with it, or at least put it up for sale, was made with opposition from my mum, and support from Sophie, though not because she wanted me to get rid.

It was with a sinking feeling I wrote-up the honest description, detailing the work that needed doing, the rust, the grotty bits, and reading it back you'd think I didn't want to sell it. It was with a sinking feeling I posted the advert to a classic car sales website and emailed the same details to the classifieds section of *Classic Car Weekly*. But there was a goal in sight, and that's why Sophie was supportive.

On one hand, selling my first classic — a decent runner, and a fun car to drive, knowing there wouldn't be another functioning classic car in my own garage until God-knows-when, honestly filled me with dread. On the other, keeping it would mean accepting Maggie wouldn't get finished, despite how bad things had become, and also mean I wouldn't have funds to pay for the work in progress. I listed it for what I paid — £2,250, thinking if a buyer wanted to knock ten per cent off I would get enough to cover my next bill.

In some respects, I was really lucky. I had one or two calls making enquiries but the first person who came to view the Midget ended-up buying it, for the asking price. I think the fact I was obviously going to miss it actually helped the sale, as the man who bought it could see how much fun he was going to have, and sitting in the passenger seat while he took a short test drive made me dread the fact I could tell this was the last time I would sit in this car. It was a fairly chilly but nice day, and just in case the car would be going that day I went for a short drive around Billinge to enjoy it properly one more time. As luck would have it, my sister drove past in the opposite direction and I got back to a message on my phone saying she'd seen me in my car being driven by a stranger and what on Earth was going on?

The buyer and his wife left for a chat over a coffee and, if he decided to buy it, to sort his insurance out before a very long drive of more than two hours home, which left me for half an hour at my kitchen table to think about what was happening. I thought I'd made my peace with the decision, and kept reminding myself that this was just another step on the long road to having the Magnette in working order while also relieving me of the responsibility of caring for another classic car while the Maggie project lurched from one problem to another. It still gave me bad butterflies though.

A smiling man knocked on my door and I knew for sure that was the Midget gone. He paid the asking price, despite me pointing out every bit of rust, and a repair section that hadn't been painted, leaving a patch of grey primer visible among the vermillion (the MG name for orange) metalwork by the rear wheel, before the test drive, and he transferred the money there and then.

I handed him the keys.

'Don't follow me out,' he said with a sympathetic smile. 'I know how this feels.'

I wouldn't say I was close to crying, but I was gutted. I shook his hand and wished him happy motoring then sat at the kitchen table, listening for the car to start up and leave my life. He had no problems starting it, the advantage of it being warmed-up, and I heard it gently rev and drive away. With a heavy sigh I ventured out to the drive to close the door on my empty garage.

There was also the pressing matter of having a BMW we were growing to dislike, and after an expensive incident weeks into our ownership, the thought of future servicing and repair bills were filling us both with dread. In all honesty, the buying experience had spoiled the car for me, and I suspect Sophie, from the first day, and we just wanted rid. Luckily, my brother-in-law had a solution to offer. He had a 2010 Vauxhall Insignia which he no longer needed and was selling — and would sell cheaply to us. My plan was to palm the BMW off to a dealer, use some of the cash to buy the Insignia and use the rest to settle what was left of the loan I took out when I cancelled the finance on the BMW. I'd file the little bit we'd already paid off the loan under 'expensive lessons learned' and we'd basically be back to where we started with a car which was cheaper to run. I was fortunate that a dealer would pay us enough for the BMW to carry-out my plan, and that would save me from the tyre kickers selling it myself would attract, though it didn't stop me being nervous as hell when the salesperson took it out for a test drive. Now would be an opportune moment for the since-repaired car to throw up its dreaded Drive Train error message again. Thankfully, it didn't.

'Lovely to drive, isn't it,' she said as she walked back into the showroom while I was swilling around the dregs of a machine-made coffee in a disposable cup.

I nodded and tried not to hand the spare key over to her too quickly, as I leaned over to sign the form. The money would be in my account by the end of the day. I just had an image in my mind of the error message popping up after I'd left and getting a call to tell me no money would be coming my way. I've never checked my bank account so often in such a short space of time.

I happily got the bus home from work that evening with the worst car-buying experience of my life behind me, and my brother-in-law called round with the Insignia that evening for us to take out on a test drive to make sure we were happy before transferring him the money. As usual with a new car, I quickly got it kitted-out with some new boots and we were good to go. I've never owned a car under the age of 35 I've liked so much.

17

Admitting Defeat

Beauford Tourer
If you've been to a wedding, you've seen a Beauford. Respectfully, the wedding car of choice for non-car enthusiasts. They were first built by the Beauford Car Company in the 1980s and are styled to look like 1930s cars, but with the reliability of having modern running gear. Not for us.

With our engagement, a tentative start at looking for a wedding venue had been put on hold because my remaining grandparents kept dying. It sort of kills the mood a little bit. I doubt either would have wanted us to put any plans on hold, but it does, whether you'd want them to or not, and if I wasn't in the mood to be shown around country houses and to be asked to decide whether to have duck or beef then the guests from my family probably wouldn't be in the mood to traipse around John Lewis for outfits. By April 2018, around 11 months since my mum called me after that dreaded visit to her dad's house, we were just about feeling okay about resuming our wedding planning.

The only caveat was I — we — had no spare money. Well, not enough to pay for a decent wedding and the only savings I had were accounted for. I had the money from the sale of my Midget, and a shade over two grand would probably only cover the flowers anyway. The cost of a wedding is eye-watering and I can only imagine what people must have gone through post-Covid and in the midst of a cost of living crisis if they want to have any sort of wedding.

The latest round of work on the Magnette had just reached a close, with the bill at £2,964 for 47 hours of work completed between 12th March, 2018 and 2nd May, plus extras such as paint, welding materials and stone chip protection.

Work in those 47 hours included welding the offside floorpan (where there was no floor any more), starting work on cutting away rusty bits on the nearside (passenger side) and carrying on working on the engine. It was now fully cleaned, rebuilt and painted. It just needed to be reunited with the car once the welding work was complete.

After the £2,250 I'd managed to get for the Midget, there really was no money left after I'd gone a handful of months with basically no disposable income to make up the other £700 needed to cover the bill, and with nothing left in the pot, and having used what I'd determined was the very last of my extra lives from my mum, I asked Quest to stop work altogether. Maggie needed to come home.

This was a tough decision to make emotionally as it meant admitting she would, in all likelihood, not be our wedding car. A big part of starting the project in the first place was the prospect of a grand unveiling taking Sophie and her dad to our wedding venue, playing the same role for us as it did for my mum and dad and adding to a sentimental family story.

Realistically it wasn't a decision. It was to carry on with the car or start saving for a wedding. There was no way it could be both. Not if we were going to get married any time soon.

The plus side was it did mean we would no longer be restricted to wedding venues within easy reach of a car that would be 63 years old and had not moved under its own steam in 36 of those. That meant, for us, there was only one place that was going to be a serious contender.

We'd expanded our search into Scotland and started by looking at — and provisionally booking — a venue near Newton Stewart, which we'd chosen to look at while staying at a tiny cottage which had beautiful walks for the dog and amazing views at night. At one point we were talking about trailering the Magnette to Scotland to ensure it would actually make it that far without me having to set off three days early to crawl up to and past the border without using a motorway and allowing for breakdowns. This plan was curtailed when the owners of the venue decided they weren't hosting weddings any more and with that, Sophie looked up from the computer screen one night when we were scouring venues and said: 'Shall we just look in Edinburgh?'

It made perfect sense. Ever since I booked a trip to the Scottish capital for Sophie's birthday to impress her when our relationship was only a few months old, it has been a special place for us, and we averaged going back at least once a year, sometimes three, before covid and kids. When I'm not under the reassuring gaze of Winter Hill in the North West of England, it is the place I next feel most like I'm at home. This plan also had the added bonus of necessitating a trip to Edinburgh to view venues. This meant lots of food in our favourite restaurants, and a night or two of having a few too many and walking off hangovers in the Scottish National Gallery in-between the serious business of finding a venue. There was suddenly a lot of pressure on the city — and us — as I think we liked the idea so much we were desperate for it to happen.

We needn't have worried. After only a handful of viewings we were left with the Signet Library on Parliament Square and the Royal Botanic Garden, with the Botanics winning the vote thanks to it having, among a few other things, more space for photos and therefore a bigger capacity for those photographs to not have tourists lurking in the background of them. We also loved the idea of getting married outside, which you couldn't do at the time in England, and two Redwood trees at the Botanics were where we'd planned the action. The date was set, and in all honesty I wasn't even thinking about the car until we got home.

When we did get home, it was pretty hard NOT to think about the car. It was strewn over two garages — mine and my mum's, and whichever garage you looked into, there was little cause for hope that all the bits would be reunited as a single car anytime in the foreseeable future.

18

A Wedding, Without the Car

1965 Daimler 250 V8
Sharing a body with the MKII Jaguar means onlookers can be forgiven for mistaking one of these for a 'Morse'.

The main differences lie in the engine, with the Jag using a straight six. A squeeze in the back, the car can actually take four passengers, with one in the front, though many brides would probably not appreciate the overcrowding.

At our house was a half-welded car, which was solid as a bus on the driver's side and still precariously crusty on the other. With no seats and exposed metal and primer where new metal had been let in, the grey contrasting with the black made it look every bit a project car. All that was missing was the bits of garden furniture and children's toys many of these projects accumulate as they take on a new role as a makeshift storage compartment. It looked like it was never going to get finished — any day now the neighbours would start asking what I planned to do with it.

Meanwhile, at my mum's house, the seats and bits of the interior were still carefully stacked and wrapped in her garage, but now they were joined by a newly-built, clean and pristinely-painted engine. I went for maroon and black and it looked amazing. After painting, Quest had even carefully put back the engine ID plates. The only issue was the engine had no car to go in.

Even with the car back, I couldn't reunite the shell with the interior because the passenger side needed a lot of welding, and that was pretty much all my skills allowed for at this point. It had literally stalled the project as wedding planning took hold.

Now the venue was in place, it was obvious that the Magnette wasn't going to be finished for our date in July, 2019, and it was obvious that even if it were possible, Edinburgh would be a step too far. Finding an appropriately classic-oriented car hire firm was fortunately no problem, Edinburgh Classic Wedding Cars appeared to do exactly what it said on the tin, and they have a beautiful 1965 Daimler 250 V8 in their stable. I was more than happy to take responsibility for transport on the day, though I really don't think Sophie cared much about what she would arrive in. But it mattered a great deal to me. If it couldn't be Maggie, it had to be something good i.e. not a Beauford, and with my dad being such a huge Daimler fan, it was a subtle nod to him, as for obvious reasons he wouldn't be there.

John at Edinburgh Classic Wedding Cars was sympathetic to my situation, and happily the Daimler was available. I'd probably only get to see it for a few minutes after the ceremony, but that wasn't what was important to me. My bride would arrive at her wedding in a proper car, and I had managed to facilitate that. No one would see her and her dad go past them on the day and cause them to tut at the choice of car.

While I was on the case, I decided to take my Minister for Transport title for the wedding a little further, and discovered a company called The Red Bus, which hires classic London Routemaster buses to ferry people around Edinburgh. I did the digging after Sophie and I saw one in action during our trip to the city to look for a venue, and even though we only wanted a handful of guests to be taken the ten minutes down the road from The Bonham Hotel to the gardens, it was a few hundred quid well spent — though I tried not to think about the wiring loom for a ZA which could have been bought with the funds.

As the months ticked down towards the wedding, the ZA, despite confronting me every time I opened the garage, didn't weigh me down as much as I had expected it to. When we started the project of getting it back on the road, the Magnette being our wedding car one day was my top priority. I did, at the time, find accepting it wouldn't be ready really hard, but then I had to ask myself what were the most important things when it came to the wedding, and if having the car there was a good enough reason to put it off. As it turned out, we'd look back on our wedding with a couple of reasons to be glad we didn't wait.

Not having my dad at the wedding was one of the reasons I was so keen to have Maggie there, but just as wedding planning got started, we were hit with a possibility none of us wanted to go near discussing. Sophie's dad was diagnosed with lung cancer, which necessitated the removal of a lung and nearly killed him. With this going on, planning a wedding naturally became less enjoyable for a time, though the suggestion of cancelling was quickly dismissed as one; it meant admitting there was a reason to cancel the wedding when we hoped he would survive and be well enough to walk Sophie down the aisle and two; no one would say this but if we were running against the clock then delaying the wedding wouldn't achieve anything.

I often wonder how he felt at the time, having only recently recovered from such major surgery, but by early 2019 we were more hopeful by the week that everything would be alright, and by April we were confident enough to book our honeymoon — to Hong Kong followed by Bali — the definition of a once-in-a-lifetime trip.

And one that seemed very irresponsible given I was about to quit my full time job to become a student again.

Not having a degree had been one of the biggest itches I'd wanted to scratch since I was about 23 and had decided it was too late to go to university. For someone who was always seen as one of the clever ones at school, and who found it easy to get good GCSE results, it was probably expected I'd take a traditional path to university. But I fell off a cliff when I was supposed to be working for my A Levels. I went to Winstanley College on the outskirts of Wigan, and it carried a reputation for being one of the best state sixth forms in the country at the time and still is highly-ranked. With GCSEs like mine, I was expected to find my A Levels a breeze, but, and this was entirely my fault, I spent too much time in the smoking shelter and too much time thinking supporting Bon Jovi would see me through, and not enough time actually showing any interest in my subjects. In the end I did get offered a place at Manchester Metropolitan University, but by then I'd missed all my student finance deadlines and had made no preparations to actually apply myself to any studies. My parents even offered to pay my fees so I could go it without a loan, but I instead opted to go to work. In hindsight that was probably the right move at the time as I was in no fit state to occupy a university place that someone else would have deserved more, but as I got older it was very much a source of real regret.

My wanting to study had been something Sophie had always been supportive of, and while the feeling subsided a lot when I first started my career in journalism, it gradually came back, to the point where she decided we should look if we could do it. It turned-out, if we really tightened our belts and I borrowed the most I could from a student loan, we could just about manage a year, long enough for me to do a Master's.

That would be, of course, without having a wedding and a car restoration to pay for, but what I did have was a very generous mum, who handed-on some of what my dad's dad had left when he died to each of us. My decision was made by March 2019, and I applied to study for my MA in Broadcast Journalism, which they accepted me onto having decided my professional experience would be enough to meet the entry requirements, seeing that my route was far from traditional. It was definitely the scenic route into higher education, or what my dad would have called 'the pretty way.'

The plan was to work up until the wedding, have August to enjoy our honeymoon and start freelancing, and then start my course in the September, with a view to going into a broadcast job once I'd graduated. My inheritance, plus student loan, would just about see us through, even though it was definitely a gamble. Having said that, I never thought for a minute — perhaps foolishly — that I'd be struggling for a job come September 2020.

Come July Sophie's dad's recovery seemed complete. After a downpour of biblical proportions on the morning of 20th July, 2019 moved our wedding from under the Redwoods to inside, the sun came out in time for the ceremony and Sophie arrived, with her dad, in the Daimler. The Routemaster also played its small role so I was happy with my little contribution to the day's transport, though not with what I did to Sophie's car a couple of days later.

We stayed on in Edinburgh for a couple of days after the wedding, mainly to register the marriage at the office on the Royal Mile before going home. We also needed to return to the Botanics to pick up some decorations.

By this time, Sophie had bought her own car for work (another Insignia as we liked mine so much) and we were using this for the trip up to Scotland. We'd only had the car about four months and it was still new, without even a swirl mark on it, so it was up to me as the car enthusiast to take a very tight angle out of the car park at The Bonham and scrape half the driver's side against a tiny, but very sturdy, bollard. It was a good job we'd only been married a couple of days as I think that fact may have diluted any potential argument somewhat. I knew when I heard the crunch that it was going to be more than just a scratch and it was purely because I was being an idiot that it happened. I should have realised the angle was too tight before turning out of the car park (it's a tight exit anyway, but doable) and I could have backed up and started again. Instead, I tried to go forwards and there was no going back once contact had been made. It was an ugly scrape, and one which cost me an unbudgeted £400 once we'd got home. That would have made a very decent dent in parts which would be needed for Maggie if the welding ever got finished.

There wasn't a great deal of thinking about the car to be done though, if I'm honest, because we pretty much went away straight away once we were home. We arrived in Edinburgh on the Friday, got married on the Saturday and left on the Monday, before flying to Hong Kong on the Wednesday and only returning home just over two weeks after that.

Usually when we're on holiday I stumble across at least a couple of wishlist cars, but the trendy SUVs of Hong Kong didn't touch the sides like the Trabants and Ladas on a previous trip to Budapest did. I remember once, while sitting in a beer garden with a very good friend, Wigan sports editor and now journalism tutor Phil Wilkinson, a Ferrari went past and it was followed by a Vauxhall Viva (a proper one). Phil turned to me and said: 'I know which one you'd prefer,' and he was right. He meant it as a jibe, but we like what we like. I will admit that I saw a handful of cars I wouldn't say no to at a McLaren showroom while out walking in Hong Kong, after travelling on the two modes of transport on the planet I am afraid of — cable trams and cable cars.

The Peak Tram, which has been running since 1888, was, my quick Googling tells me, the first funicular railway in Asia. That means the tram is hauled up the slope via a cable. For those who haven't been on it, the views as you ascend the slope of the harbour are incredible, but these are accompanied by the nagging feeling the cable may break. I obviously didn't say anything to Sophie, who was happily making me pose for selfies and generally enjoying her day. It was only when we boarded a glass-bottomed cable car to Lantau Island to see the big Buddah I casually told her I was a little scared of our chosen mode of transport.

'Why did you pay extra for one with a glass bottom then?'

The real answer is because even though I was terrified, I found the opportunity to conquer my fear by boarding a near-six kilometre cable car ride lasting more than 20 minutes, much of it over water, absolutely fascinating. I knew I wasn't going to cause a scene, and at worst I'd spend 18 minutes or so in a private state of panic, and if I did manage to enjoy it, the views would be incredible, and they were. (Although I was really thinking the worst that could happen would be that the cable would break and I'd be proved right).

A lack of car reminders followed us to Bali. After waiting what felt like hours to get through immigration (and I was pulled to one side to have my bags searched and pockets turned-out) our car could barely move through the traffic as the road, in both directions, was taken up by mopeds doing what looked like their own thing, and even though I've wanted a motorbike for a long time I decided we wouldn't be hiring a scooter to join them. There were people with babies strapped to them and toddlers holding on at the back and sitting over handlebars as they weaved and darted past other people on bikes holding ladders and pets. That wasn't what I found most interesting though. The fact you could buy petrol from carts on the side of the road, in makeshift containers such as vodka bottles, was one of my favourite things to look out for and take photos of. Petrol stations, once out of the main towns, are few and far between in Bali, so these shacks, called Warungs, sell everything from groceries to petrol. The petrol ones are sometimes in front of garages with scooters undergoing various states of servicing and the litre bottles sell for about 40p. If I did have to buy petrol though, I'd be wondering exactly how much petrol came in those litre bottles and how much was topped-up with something else.

There are a few moments in life, I think if you're lucky, where you can be granted a stretch of time without worry or pressures of work, and it was doubly so for me as, at the age of 31, I was coming home to go back to school instead of work. During the trip home, the closest I got to worry was us almost missing our connection from Hong Kong to Manchester. We'd arrived at Bali airport in plenty of time for our flight, and about 10 minutes before we were due to board, an announcement came over the tannoy to say that if our flight took off now it would land in Hong Kong a lot earlier than the scheduled time, so we weren't going to leave for a while. I think the 'delay' was around 30 minutes. Everyone seemed fine, but quietly a little bit of panic was setting in for me as we made use of the time by chipping into more of what was left of our holiday smokes.

In fact, the first time I thought this may have been a problem was when we were booking our honeymoon, and the agent was telling us that on the way home we'd land in Hong Kong two hours and 55 minutes before we were scheduled to take off for Manchester. I don't know why I didn't say anything at the time, but very quietly, underneath the hubbub of everything going on in my brain, this minor detail was tugging my attention like a person waving their arms at the back of a noisy crowd ever since the holiday proposal was sent to us 12 months before.

Of course, we ended up being delayed properly. After squeezing one last holiday beer in (we'd tried to avoid cliche chains, so it was at the airport's Hard Rock Cafe and paying normal prices for a beer was a shock after nearly two weeks on Bintang). Once we'd boarded the plane we taxied forever. It turned out our new take-off time was a sought-after slot, and we landed in Hong Kong five minutes before our flight was scheduled to leave for Manchester. I'm only exaggerating a bit, it was more like seven minutes. Thankfully, the best in people travelling came out once the plane was down, which was especially nice as in my experience planes bring out the very worst in people. There was one Ryanair flight to Barcelona, in 2017 among all the shit that was going on at home, and Sophie and I had a short holiday booked before it all kicked off and we went anyway. On our flight was a group of young lads obviously on a first holiday without their parents. There were maybe 30 of them and I could tell we were in for a bumpy flight when they were falling over in the bar pre-7.00am. They spent the flight shouting, fighting, pushing past staff trying to help people and generally being twats. I remember spending two thirds of the flight needing a wee and not being able to leave my seat because they were all piled up in the aisle — it was so bad the captain even apologised over the tannoy when we landed, but to my satisfaction we were on the same flight home as a handful of them and they were very sheepish and one had a black eye any prop forward would have been proud of. (And we'd had a lovely time).

There's also all the barging in queues and the rush from everyone to get up and grab their bags to be first off the plane. I'd never understood that, as I was always of the opinion that it wouldn't result in getting anywhere any faster because of passport queues, waiting for baggage and the like. Until now.

There were obviously others on the flight who were also planning to zoom through to try and make it onto the same Manchester flight we'd given up on, but word was passed round the plane and the passengers who weren't attempting a mad dash either stayed put or made way for those of us about to run, ignoring the shouted and desperate calls from airport staff that running was not allowed in the airport, despite how empty it was.

In the end we needn't have run. The flight waited for us as it turns out most people leaving for Manchester from Hong Kong at 1am were connecting from various Indonesian islands. Even better, when we boarded, the person sitting next to me got up and moved, never to return. I can't remember if I offered Sophie the extra seat (I have a feeling you'll get different accounts from each of us) but I do know I lifted the armrest up, lay flat and slept for most of the flight. An upgrade to the next class up wouldn't have been as comfortable. The only major downside was that our bags were 24 hours behind us, but not having two cases of dirty washing to deal with on the comedown from a once-in-a-lifetime trip wasn't too much hassle.

But not having to go back to work did a lot in diluting those end-of-holiday blues, though stupidly, crazily as my only income was a student loan and my capital from my inheritance was very much finite, I called Quest.

Once again, on September 3rd, 2019, the Magnette was pushed into the sunlight from the safety of my garage. It was easy to do since there was no interior and no engine, and I took a picture while waiting for Sonny from Quest to arrive with the low loader to winch it on. I wondered if the neighbours were thinking I'd finally decided to sell it, given I was out of work to study.

'Self-unemployed' I called it.

With some inheritance earmarked for the car, I didn't really think about not asking them to start work again. I'd backed myself to get a job by September 2020 and set up a standing order to feed our bills account with just enough money for 12 months. There was money for the car, and then if I made anything freelancing that could be my beer money. I realised then, as I do now, it was a privileged position to be in, and I'm not entirely sure I'd make the same decisions again given the opportunity. Knowing now what happened in the months after this, I think I'd have kept more money back.

But in September 2019 I didn't know the world was going to grind to a halt six months later.

I also didn't know we'd be expecting our first child, though that wasn't really a consideration as we'd semi-planned for it to be on the cards shortly after the wedding. And babies don't cost a lot while they're getting ready to be born if you take things out of the equation such as decorating their bedroom, buying clothes, furniture and things to transport them in such as prams and car seats. OK, babies cost a lot before they are born.

In September 2019, our baby wasn't even a pre-baby and the word 'zoom' was still mainly used as an onomatopoeia. In just six weeks the unwelded side was done, and it was as bad as I'd feared. The passenger side of the car had been on the side of my mum's garage where there was a side door, and my theory is that for three decades of the car standing still, moisture being let in from the slight gaps around the door had very slowly worked its magic on that side of the car to make all the metal resemble a teabag. Shortly after Maggie had left mine, I was invited to Quest to take a look at what needed doing.

Seeing the passenger side braced, and a corroded floor pan and lower wing section on the ground was about as sorry a sight as I thought I was ever going to see until a gloved hand demonstrated to me how pretty much all of the sill could be removed with minimal force. But we decided to persevere, not just because stopping now would have resulted in a huge waste of time (and money) but also because of the lethal dose of sentimental value the car holds.

Repair sections to the front inner wheel arch, front floor and passenger wing were fabricated and fitted along with new sills. Corrosion repairs and structural repairs to the underside were also done. Once all this was finished the underside was cleaned, rust treated and primed, with the odd filler repair for areas where the diminishing budget called for a 'get it done and come back to it later' approach. The rest — I hoped — was cosmetic.

Granted, the door bottoms could really have done with some attention, but as far as the rest of the car and its paintwork went, I wanted to the car to look the 63 years old it was at the time.

We also made a start on putting various bits back together. The front suspension was stripped, cleaned and reassembled along with the clutch secondary cylinder, rear brakes and fuel lines. The engine, rebuilt more than a year ago at this point, was picked up from my mum's garage and reunited with the car, though it wasn't yet plumbed-in.

And with student life giving me some free time, I spent it sourcing everything from a new exhaust system and brake master cylinder to oil filters and spark plugs, which were left to sit in boxes waiting for their turn to contribute to the project.

I also threw the wheels into the boot of my workhorse Vauxhall Insignia (an unlikely candidate for a future classic given it is always one of at least three in any queue of traffic) and got new tyres fitted.

The tyre fitter remembered the Firestones which were on the wheels being launched in the late 1970s, which tells you how old the tyres were, and with fresh boots we now had a car that could be rolled in and out of my garage without much resistance.

All this work, plus materials and consumables, came across two invoices. One for an eye-watering £5,148 and another, also eye-watering, for £2,958. I would have said it was the fastest I'd ever spent eight grand in my life, but I'd just had a wedding. As you'll be able to guess from those figures, the payments came to more than I'd budgeted in my head, and looking back I'd have enjoyed my first semester at university so much more without such a huge financial burden so early in my studies. I know it was self-imposed and the last thing I seek is sympathy. I'm more looking to making the point that attaching sentimentality to an object skews your willingness to make sensible decisions.

Anyway, with most of my cash now spent on yet more welding and some student loan also now in car-form, after paying the second of the two invoices, on 15th October, 2019, it was time again for a break.

19

Another Bump in the Road

Mamas and Papas Ocarro pram
Top speed: 100mph down a hill while making car noises and after catching your breath
0-60: Depends how long you've had to catch your breath
Economy: Quite good, can run on a person fuelled by a burger and two pints
Cost when new: £759 (I know).

It will sound strange when you consider Sophie found out she was pregnant halfway through my year of self-unemployment that our first child was planned.

We were approaching our seventh anniversary-ish (we don't have a date set in stone) and we always knew that once we'd had a good run of holidays and all-nighters we'd like to settle into parenthood. It was strange really. As a perpetual worrier it would seem I would want to be more than 1,000 per cent sure of a job before committing to something as serious as having a dependant, but I was never worried about that. I've always taken the view that if you wait until you're financially secure enough to have children then you'll never have them. It's never a good time, so you may as well get on with it.

My tendency is to worry about things completely out of my control. Big exam? No problem, if I work for it, I'll get the grade. Job interview? I can prepare, be sharp and perform well. The welfare of my unborn child? Well, you may as well stay awake all night and think about everything that can go wrong. Interest rates? Yes, let's have it. I'll ponder those at 3am while I'm also reading about all the things that can go wrong during a birth.

To be honest it's completely knackering. Put a knife in the drawer the wrong way round? Don't you dare — someone will die. It's probably my way of trying to maintain some form of control in an unpredictable world. I'll do things like not allow myself to scratch an itch until five minutes have passed or I'll stir my coffee exactly 100 times clockwise and then 50 times anti-clockwise (a habit I've, thankfully, broken). Some days are quieter than others, but this, along with the tendency to catastrophise things out of my control, sometimes put me in a funk. I've spoken to people about it, I should probably do so again. I've had thoughts like this for as long as I can remember and was definitely a child when it started.

One thing that wasn't easy to avoid catastrophising about was Sophie's dad. After being well and walking her down the aisle in the July, by November 2019 his cancer was back, in his brain. The kick between the legs from this one (as opposed to my dad) was so different because we were all so hopeful he would have enjoyed years, not weeks, of better health. One thing Sophie and I always said to each other was 'he'll meet our kids' and now this hope was hanging by a thread. As was typical of him, he was good-humoured, if not always positive. His response to me setting-up a collection to go towards treatment abroad, which his partner had researched, was met with: "You better not shave your beard off," and as he knew Sophie's sister was looking at October 2020 for her wedding date, he said: 'Objective one; live until next October.' Our approach was to try and be as normal as we could. Sophie's dad's prognosis was still in its infancy and there was little any of us could do until we knew more.

Being a student gave me more time at home than I was used to, and I filled the days I wasn't on campus by doing some odds and sods such as writing for *Classic Car Weekly*, and doing the bits on the ZA I could. Now the bodywork was done, I could get to grips with a few little bits of mechanicals as well as putting the interior back in. The people at Quest were honest and said I could save a bit of money by doing some of the jobs myself while I had the car back, but to be honest it wasn't as much about saving a few quid as it was me wanting to do a portion of the work myself. Alright, I was never going to put an interior back in a car as well as a professional, but I wanted to say I'd done it, and learn some lessons along the way.

In the November, me and a friend, former journalist colleague Gary Brunskill, started the first of our 'playing cars' days. Gary, a photographer for the Wigan papers, and the *St Helens Reporter* back when that not only just existed, but thrived, is a fellow car enthusiast. I like seeing Gary because he calms me down, and us mucking about on the drive fixing cars or chatting over a brew on the dining table are some of the times the volume on that worry in my mind gets turned down. 'Respond, don't react,' is one of his, and a piece of advice I try — and fail — to adhere to.

I wheeled the car out into the drive for the first of our cold winter's days playing out and shifted the boxes containing bits of trim and knackered carpet. Buying new wasn't something I wanted to entertain. As far as I am aware the interior is original, possibly even the carpets, and even if it had been replaced at some stage, I didn't want new. It wasn't even about preserving originality as such. When something needs replacing, it needs replacing. But equally, if it doesn't, let it wear its age.

We started by laying the carpets out on the garage floor and using the new Dyson someone bought Sophie and I as a wedding present to hoover 30-odd years of dirt and fluff out of them, before laying it out like a jigsaw to work out which bit was supposed to go where, as well as the various bits of soundproofing material.

I am 100 per cent certain a lot of the soundproofing material didn't go back, or went back in the wrong place, because we had some left over when we had laid it down and stuck it back into place with carpet glue, but the faded maroon carpets were less trouble. The wear on the driver's side where the pedals had touched the carpet over the years contrasted with the less work the passenger side had been asked to do over the years. Some of the carpet to go in the back was in much better condition, and parts of it are a much deeper shade of maroon where it has been protected from the sun by a seat. It's those little signatures of this car I wanted to preserve, and I was happy in the hue of aerosol glue, instant coffee and a slightly chilly but bright morning, as Gary downed tools and told me it was time for a pie run. There's a Greggs about ten minutes' walk from the house, but we tended to go for Galloways, which required the same amount of time but required a drive, at the bottom end of Billinge, as Greggs don't do pies and I prefer Galloways pastry.

My mum was pleased too, on November 18th, 2019, the interior finally left her garage and Gary and I started refitting the seats and screwing various rails into place.

Once the carpets, and most of the soundproofing, were down, the back bench seat was a doddle to slot into place. The driver's seat, which Gary assessed as being a two-brew job, had other ideas, though. I hadn't taken the seats out, and a photograph of what the seat slotted into the rail would look like when fitted, if it existed, would be on one of the CDs Quest had sent to me. The only device I had that would read a CD was a ten-year-old laptop that takes about an hour to start-up, and another hour to read the disc. The brews would have been very cold by this point.

There are more screw holes in the floor than there are in the seat rails, which made finding exactly how the rails went back a bit of a guessing game. Fortunately, there were deep dents in the carpet where the rails had previously been, and this led to only one possible combination of holes. We also knew for sure that the carpets were the right way around because of the rubber mat fixed into the driver's side carpet. But once the rails were screwed on, there appeared to be no way to get the seat onto it. Sliding the driver's seat on from the front seemed impossible without taking the steering wheel out, because there just wasn't enough space, and screwing the rail to the one attached to the seat before putting it in the car meant there would be no access to the holes to screw the rails to the floor of the car. We were utterly stumped and ended-up leaving it to sleep on, which is rare as neither of us like a job to flummox us.

The answer, in the end, was brute force. Another way we tried to put the seats back was by sitting on the bench set at the back and pushing it forwards, but doing it this way always seemed to leave it stuck about halfway along. I was adamant we were putting the right seat back in the right place, because there is a tear in the passenger seat which I remember always being there, and it does matter which way around they go because there is a slight cutout in each seat which goes along the drive shaft tunnel. Just to be sure, we switched them around and tried that, but sure enough they wouldn't fit.

On December 4, 2019 (I know because I checked on my phone as I took a picture) I tried that tack again, only I was much more firm with my pushing of the seat. I was a bit kind the first time, not waiting to do any damage to a seat more than twice my own age, but for some reason I just went for it this time, using the back seat to wedge my body in place while I used my weight to slide the seat forwards. And it worked. Immediately thinking I must have done something wrong, I leapt out of the car and jumped back in the front to test the rail. The seat clicked into place and would slide back and forth on a lift of the leaver, but stayed put once I let go. I pushed my feet into the floor and pushed back. The seat didn't move. I don't know how I managed this, but the fact I'd managed it gave me a huge boost. It's daft how something as simple as fitting a seat to your car can lift you, but after being so disheartened a few days before, something so simple really made it feel like the whole project was back on track. Once the driver's seat was back in place, the passenger seat went in without any protest at all, but I decided not to tell Gary of my triumph, but wait for him to get in touch with me. I wanted to show him my achievement, and his next visit wasn't wasted. We had more trim to fit to reach a natural stopping point before Christmas and my planned trip to Edinburgh with Sophie in the build-up.

We'd had a family Christmas in Ely, with Sophie's dad and his partner sharing the table with Sophie's mum, her partner, and Sophie's sisters and their other halves. It was obvious Sophie's dad wasn't well, but what we didn't expect was him to be dead six weeks later. The laughter, the wine, the food and gift of a new case to pack his things to go to a flat he'd bought in Fuerteventura all suggested death wasn't quite so close. We were either blind or in denial, at least outwardly, and I'm grateful for that because he spent his last Christmas with his family and no one was thinking about his funeral. We were also hoping happier things would soon occupy our thoughts.

And I knew on New Year's Day.

There was a classic car meet every New Year's Day at the now closed Corner House pub in Wrightington. With my Midget sold and the Magnette not ready, Gary picked me up in his Midget, flask of tea made up and camping chairs in the boot. It's essentially sitting in the cold with bacon butties and cups of tea and talking cars. Sophie wanted me to see Gary and we'd had a quiet New Year's Eve. I was good for the 8.00am pick-up.

I just knew something was different though. It sounds silly, and it looks silly seeing it written down, but magpies can play a role with me trying to find order in the chaos of the universe, and while I know it has no correlation to life, I'll salute lone magpies and be pleased when I see two.

One of the things I love about the drive to Wrightington on New Year's Day at that time is how quiet the roads are. It's not quite light and there's a sense everyone behind every drawn curtain you drive past is not long into their sleep. It's quite soothing. And as we rounded a corner four magpies scattered and flew away from the middle of the road. I thought 'well then, Sophie's pregnant and she's having a boy.'

Two days later, while I was trying to fix a kitchen cupboard to distract myself from the agonising wait for confirmation, Sophie calmly turned the pregnancy test screen towards me with a, 'Well there you go.'

After spending the previous few months trying to distract ourselves from bad family news, learning we were going to become parents was lovely, but it also felt so normal. I had always wanted to be a parent, though until then I had acknowledged I wasn't ready (are we ever?) and my excitement was accompanied by an equal amount of worry. I was scared of what could happen, rather than focusing on the nice bits, and looking back I wish I could have just enjoyed the moment rather than expecting something would go wrong, or that the scan would bring terrible news of some kind.

We also made sure we told Sophie's dad. We hoped he'd meet our baby, and at the time, despite how serious his condition was, we really didn't expect him not to. Telling him early was more of a 'just in case,' or at least it was to my mind. I don't know if we were right to be hopeful, or if it was ignorant on our part, or if I didn't want to confront what was happening (I can't speak for Sophie on this).

And he didn't meet our baby.

Sophie's dad's deterioration was sudden, and his death quick. We'd visited him at home to tell him our news, then again at hospital the following week, when he told us he was being moved to a hospice. The following week we went to the hospice to see him, and the following morning he was dead. It was early February, 2020.

It was an honour to be a pallbearer for him, though coffins are always heavy and as well as being the first one I carried on my left shoulder, there was the added burden of worrying about my newly-pregnant wife, grieving for her dad.

It was horrible. I know people say you should think about happy memories and celebrate people's lives at funerals, but people dying is crap — it doesn't matter that it happens to everybody — and funerals aren't nice. Anyone can say that they want their funeral to be an occasion where people talk about happy memories and wear bright colours and that's fine, but if you feel sad you should also be allowed to wear black and cry and acknowledge that feeling of a huge great hole where the middle of your body once was.

But we got through it. Sophie let me hold her, and she cried, but she was also amazing. And her friends, Clare and James, were also amazing, driving up to Oakham from London for the day just to be with her. And then we went home the following day to our lives and Sophie's pregnancy. I was so grateful we had something so huge to look forward to, even if worrying the baby and if my wife would be OK was keeping me awake some nights.

The end of February brought the reassurance of our first scan, and right up to the point of the sonographer turning the monitor on I had a lump in my throat. Then the picture of a moving baby appeared and, for the first time since we found out, I relaxed. I don't remember much else about the day, other than we were waiting a long time for the scan once we arrived and I remember going to the machine to buy the printouts. I got two for us and one each for our mums, and I told my mum she could finally start sharing our news. Knowing how I feel about posting pictures of other people's children on social media, my mum posted a picture on Facebook of the card the picture of the scan came in. I found it funny that she thought I'd apply the same rule to a scan.

Despite the obvious pain Sophie was feeling, we were both looking forward to becoming parents, and with the recent start of my second semester at university came a student loan instalment. There was a car in the garage that needed some attention, and I promptly spent my loan money accordingly.

Everyone with an MG Magnette knows of a man called Peter Martin. He is Provider of Parts and a friendly voice at the other end of the phone when you need technical advice. I honestly don't remember how I got Peter's contact details, or who told me about him, but I will always be grateful to have him at the other end of an email or phone call.

With the car at mine and more spare time than I'd had since I was a teenager, there was only one thing for it. I was finally going to buy a wiring harness, and the fuel pump that I wished so much had been replaced when my dad and I first worked on this car.

The fuel pump was £85 and the wiring harness, a mesmerising network of every single wire the car needs, was £195. My plan was to fit the fuel pump and if not fit the wiring loom, at least thread it through. Apparently the electrical system on such cars is relatively simple, and I'll take an auto electrician's word for it. All I know is that I was a little nervous when looking at the wiring diagram in the owner's manual and even more intimidated when the harness arrived in the post two days after I'd ordered it. I decided it would be worth the extra money for the couple of hours it would take someone at Quest to do the work, and I promptly, but carefully, put it back in the box, as you would a delicate item like a nice suit, and turned my attention to the fuel pump.

The box it came in, branded SU — a well-known brand among classic car people, was printed in retro-styling and the fuel pump itself was wrapped in paper to add to the '50s feel. With everything laid out on the dining table and a free afternoon in daylight, I made sure to take pictures of where the old fuel pump was, and where various bolts went before taking it out and spilling decades-old petrol that was still in the line. Then all I had to do was clamber into the tight, dark space to put the new one in its place.

With some student loan left to burn on car stuff instead of living and paying bills, I arranged with Quest to pick the Magnette up to fit the wiring loom and start on the mechanicals — making this a running car again. The thought of spending more money was nagging me, given our situation, but there was also a new race against time. While it wasn't critical Maggie was finished in time for a wedding, it was much more so that she would be over the line by September 2020. Sophie, probably rightly, said that if Maggie wasn't finished by the time our baby was born, it would never get done. She concluded that once the baby was here, I would stop work on the car, perhaps for good, and in a few years' time we'd be right back to where we started, and the car would experience the same fate as it did in the '80s when I arrived to curtail my dad's work on the car.

During that week, we had other jobs to do. The car was collected, strapped onto the back of the low loader and off to Quest for what I hoped would be the final straight. Meanwhile, we painted the baby's room on 14th March, nearly six months before our due date because I didn't want any lingering paint fumes to affect the baby in any way (there's that OCD again). Sophie taped-up the edges (because I can't do it in a straight line) and she actually also did the majority of the painting while I did a bit and enjoyed a can of beer while taking photos of the occasion. The scene, I hope, was a lot less misogynistic than it reads. I'm just much slower at getting things done.

I still did not really believe we were going to have a tiny human completely dependent on us in a matter of months, though I'm sure Sophie would have felt differently. She was starting to show and I was bursting with pride. I was looking forward to being out, basically showing off to the world. This is my wonderful wife and we are having a baby.

But there was also an undercurrent of worry.

Since the start of the year everyone was wondering when this strange new virus was going to hit the UK, and when the first case in the country was confirmed on 28th February, the fear was it would spread like wildfire. Weirdly, for someone with a tendency to catastrophise and be anxious about literally everything, I was quite calm. I never obsessed with thoughts of loved ones being in grave danger and I never really feared for my unborn child more than I was already worrying about them as a result of what was unfolding.

After a Saturday afternoon of painting the baby's room, I went to Manchester the following Monday to work a casual shift as a shorthand tutor, and it was while there I watched then-Prime Minister Boris Johnson ask the nation to stop all non-essential travel (meaning don't go to the pub) and put pregnant women in a 'vulnerable' category of people advised to stay at home for 12 weeks. I went home and called the NHS advice line to ask if I should also stay at home, my logic being that if I was out and about then what was the point in my pregnant wife staying at home if I was just going to breeze in from a day's gallivanting in classrooms and on public transport to bring the virus sweeping through the house? The person on the other end of the phone didn't know what the advice was for me as the husband of a pregnant woman, but we agreed I should probably stay at home too.

Meanwhile, I was told the local pub was heaving that night.

The decision on whether to stay in our venture out was taken away from me anyway two days later, as universities followed suit when schools were closed indefinitely and GCSE and A-Level exams cancelled.

I will never not be amazed at how quickly my Master's course went online and how smooth the transition was. I am also grateful my assessments were mostly coursework-based and not wrapped-up in any grading controversies, because I worked damned hard on that course and I wanted the same grade as I'd have been given had Covid not struck.

And it was a matter of when, not if, we would go into a full lockdown.

As soon as it was announced that Johnson would speak to the nation on the evening of Monday 23rd March we knew what was coming. And I had a three-quarters finished car locked up in a garage three miles from home.

20

Lockdown

On foot
Top speed: About 4mph
Essential journeys only, and official advice said we were allowed to leave our homes for exercise. One hour a day should be sufficient for most people. Nobody said anything about labradors, though.

We all missed out because of lockdown. Personally, it was my time of having a designated driver. My sister had guessed Sophie was pregnant before we'd officially told everyone. We were out as a family for a meal and I was standing at the bar, when I asked for a pint of beer and a non-alcoholic cocktail with my sister in earshot. I knew she'd twigged at the time because of the face she pulled, but my sister has since said she knew at the time Sophie was pregnant because we didn't have an argument over who was going to drive home, (I'll always protest I offer to drive, though members of my family will tell a different story).

There was also the fact my Master's finished online and my car was locked up in a garage, still unfinished.

Doing a journalism qualification, or any journalism, when the world is told to stay indoors may feel impossible, but I actually found I did some of the best stuff of my career because everyone was at home. It's hard enough to secure interviews as a working journalist, and as a student the burden is felt even more. But suddenly everyone was at home with nothing to do and everyone was happy to speak on Zoom, which also allowed recording for video and audio. Granted, the sound quality isn't as good as interviewing in person, but it beats driving around spending money on diesel when you can sit in your study at home and speak to people. What I really missed was interacting with my coursemates in person. I'd always felt I'd missed out by not going to university the first time around, and when my chance did come, my experience was very different because of factors out of my control. The fact Covid had effectively ended the world also had me worrying on the work front for the first time. If the world didn't open up before September, would I get a job and would I be able to help support my new family? There was also the small matter of missing antenatal appointments.

I was desperate to see our baby at the 20-week scan at the end of April, and instead I sat in the car, along with other dads-to-be waiting for their scans as only mums were allowed into appointments in an effort to curtail the spread of infection.

I had many issues with this.

Firstly, the desired outcome of not letting me, or other dads, into such appointments, was to slow the spread of infection. We'd all been in cars with our wives and partners on the way, so anything we were carrying, they would be bringing into the appointment anyway. Secondly, as lovely as many antenatal appointments are, sometimes people are given bad news. We were lucky that it didn't happen to us, but I can imagine if you go to an appointment hoping to see a healthy baby doing some moving around and growing on a monitor and you're confronted with a different reality, I'd imagine the first person you'd need to be with, in most cases, is your partner. A mum would have to make a very long journey back to a very anxious dad after hearing the worst news on their own. Meanwhile, partners were sitting in cars for hours on end not knowing what was going on. You'd be getting more anxious by the minute, and often for no reason. In our case, everything was fine. We had a new picture of a happily growing baby and no reasons to worry. I was most upset about the fact I'd missed out on hearing the baby's heartbeat.

We ended-up paying for a private 3D scan, which we went to in June. For this one, I was allowed in, which is why we went for it. A 3D scan was never really on our agenda, but me missing hearing the heartbeat and seeing our baby again made us decide to do it, and I'm glad we did. And the pictures revealed our baby was the absolute double of Sophie's dad. I still guessed we were having a girl (I changed my mind after the magpies), but for the first time since, I had an inkling we might be having a boy.

The deadline for handing in my project for my degree came and went, I sat remote exams in politics and media law from my study and knew I'd passed them because such a big part of it had been my career for almost a decade, and Quest finally opened-up again.

The date everyone remembers is July 4th, because that's when pubs opened again, (table service only and pay by BitCoin and only sit with people you have shared a toilet with but only if you were four furlongs apart three Wednesdays ago). But for me, the date is June 25th, 2020.

Since the day after lockdown was announced, Quest sent weekly emails to everyone with projects in their hands. The first one read: 'As you will be very well aware the government has now issued a directive in relation to a UK wide temporary shutdown for non essential travel and industry.

'In order to play our part, and protect our customers, staff and community we have elected to temporarily halt operations as of this morning.

'Throughout this temporary closure we will update you weekly.

'If you are waiting for any specific information regarding your project and its progress, please be aware this may only be provided shortly after we reopen.'

Work eventually restarted in June, and with gloves and a mask, I was allowed to visit the garage on Thursday, June 25th, 2020.

In the past, I'd just waltz in whenever I was going past as Quest was so close, but I could only go now if the meeting was pre-arranged, and the usually busy workshop was quiet.

Where a handful of people would be working on a few cars, with a radio filling the quiet spaces in the background in-between the buzzes and whirring of saws, welders and the dings of heavy tools being dropped, only two people were in on this day. The smell of hot metal and old car still hung in the air, though the instant coffee didn't reach my nostrils as brews weren't allowed, and I would have probably declined the opportunity to drink out of a mug that wasn't my own anyway.

As I walked in, there was my car, in between a BMW and Mercedes which looked much more incomplete than the ZA. Maggie was without a bonnet, but the gleaming maroon and black—painted engine was back with the car, and from what I could tell, the new wiring loom had been fitted. Kel, who had done the majority of the work on my car, demonstrated the trafficator indicators, which I saw working for the first time in my life. He explained to me that the original switch, which is mounted on the steering column, wasn't working, so he'd wired them directly to the battery to show me how they worked. I could either ask him to take the entire steering column (and the wiring) out to try and fix the problem, or go for a cheaper fix. Kel knew I wanted to preserve as much originality as possible (for originality read, how the car was when my dad had it) but he also knew I was on a budget that had already gone. The cheaper option was to fit two new switches underneath the dash for me to turn each indicator on. They were period-correct, if not intended to be used as indicator switches. In the end, I reasoned that this would be my little mark on the car, so I agreed.

Then Sunny, the boss at Quest, asked me a rhetorical question.

'Would you like to hear it?'

There were still wires hanging out all over the place where the dash panel should have been (that was on the passenger seat) and there was no coolant, meaning the car could only be run for a few short seconds. It didn't matter — before Sunny and Kel had finished speaking, I was nodding frantically, ignoring their attempts to pull me back down to the ground by my ankles. 'It might not work,' they warned me. Still, they hooked the battery up to the starter and without much persuasion Maggie burst into life, and for the first time in front of my eyes.

I'd seen the telltale shake of a car rocking from side to side, trying to cough into life, before. When I was a teenager that's as far as my dad and I got. That in itself brought memories flooding back, and my stomach felt as if I'd swallowed a brick as I willed the car on for what felt like ten minutes when it was only a few seconds. Then it just happened. The roar, and it was a roar, of the 1,489cc BMC B-Series engine was what all this was for. (Side note: The ZA was the first car this engine was used in when the first ones were made in 1953). The disappointments, the nasty bills, the asking mum for money, the bumped heads and cut fingers. I wish my dad had seen it, and smelled the engine as the aroma wafted through the air in the warehouse. As much as I was desperate to 'live' this moment and not witness it first time on a phone screen, I had to record it, so I set my phone camera up and held it slightly to the side, so I could still have an organic view of what was happening, but hardly a minute after it was fired up, they had to turn it off again as an engine with no coolant soon overheats, and causing damage after a full rebuild would have been a devastating and very much avoidable setback.

I think I actually floated out of the garage, and when I sat in the driver's seat of the Insignia, I noticed how heavy my breathing was as I reached round and took my face mask off. It did, at last, feel like we were on the final straight.

With university work handed in and exams done, I spent the July looking for jobs and freelancing for *Classic Car Weekly* to keep some money coming in.

I did my exams at home, with an invigilator watching me through my webcam, and I found them to be a breeze. Yes, I should have done well in them considering journalism had been my career for a while before then, but my law exam was infinitely better because my wife also teaches the subject and was willing to help with the best form of revision available — conversation. She'd run scenarios past me when we were out walking Otis, and I'd more often than not be unable to answer fully and run them past her, repeating what she was telling me time and time again. The personal tutelage helped. I got an A.

As things started to gradually open in July, our first stop was, of course, the pub on July 4th, when the hospitality industry was allowed to open under strict rules which were never going to be conducive to these places making any money. The Holts Arms, in Billinge, has been my local forever, since I've only very briefly not lived in the village. It's been under many different landlords in the time since I've been drinking in there, about two years before my 18th birthday, but current custodian Ian Mitty is, in my humble opinion, the best. And I'm not just saying that in the hope of a pint or two.

Having been in existence since 1721, it has been closed once or twice, and badly looked after once or twice during the 10% of its lifetime I've shared with it, but since Ian took over in 2015 we have loved it, and I was scared, like everyone with a local pub, that we'd lose it due to Covid, much like I worry about the impact of the costs to keep it running that must have been spiralling in October 2022. Sophie assured me that I didn't have to feel bad about dragging her to the pub when she was seven months pregnant, because she would also be annoyed if we ever didn't have the pub to go to, and while you could argue I was perfectly capable of having a drink at home, a pint does taste different. The temperature of the cool glass felt great, and heavy, though I only had two as once we'd finished our pizza, Sophie was essentially sitting opposite me to watch me enjoy a drink while she was on the lime and soda.

While putting facemasks on and sanitising our hands was becoming second nature, progress was being made on the Magnette at the fastest pace since the project started.

As well as the wiring loom being fitted and the engine being started, all the lights were fixed, the wiper motor was replaced, new horns were fitted and everything was tested. While I was waiting, Sophie and I returned to Edinburgh for our first wedding anniversary in-between online baby classes (waste of time, maybe it's different in person). It was very strange to be in Edinburgh city centre, in July, with hardly anyone walking around. Some shops were open, but it was eerily quiet compared to what it is normally like at that time of year, when you probably wouldn't even bother going into most shops as it is so busy. Still, it was good to be back in our favourite city, and our favourite restaurants. We discovered our favourite, Taisteal, a couple of years before by me being invited to review it, and it was a difficult one to write as we enjoyed it so much.

It was another month before I really knew we were on the home straight with the car. To save a little bit of money, when Quest needed parts, instead of ordering them for me and charging me, I would source them, and as the summer went on, the parts I was being asked to buy were becoming smaller and more mundane.

We'd gone from me having to get hold of body panels, in the first instance, to me now being asked to look for things like bulbs and timing belts, and 99 times out of 100 Peter Martin would be able to provide.

Our baby's due date was approaching, and I started to wonder what would come home first, Maggie or our child, but the odds on the car shortened dramatically on August 24th when I got a call from Sunny to say I'd better tax and insure it as he was very nearly ready to take it for a test drive.

I went straight to classic car specialist Adrian Flux for my insurance, and with the small mileage and nature of the car, my premiums have been in the region of £190 each year since I've had the car back. Tax is a different matter. Vehicle Excise Duty — car tax to you and me — is £0.00 per year if your car was registered 40 or more years ago and this works on a rolling basis, meaning a new batch of cars become exempt each year. You need to apply for it when your car turns 40, and you also don't need to put it through an MOT, though you do legally need to ensure your vehicle is roadworthy. The logic behind not needing an MOT is that a lot of these cars don't have technology which is tested, mine doesn't have indicators and seatbelts, for instance. It's an arrangement not everyone is comfortable with. If you weren't a classic car enthusiast, you might Google why this is the case, and you might come across the Kwik Fit website, which states: 'This is quite a generalisation, of course, but the purpose of the MOT test is to ensure the safety of everyone on the road – the relatively small number of classic cars on the road is therefore thought to be less likely to affect general safety.' I don't know how that sits with you, but the wording of this makes me feel uneasy.

My own view is that regardless of how much someone might enjoy looking after their car, in some cases human nature is bound to take over and some owners may cut corners if there is no obligation to get their car through a test. Knowing a car needs work doing and that work will cost a couple of hundred quid should make people stay off the road until such work is done, but a quick nip to the shops to keep everything moving is bound to happen. There are also well-meaning enthusiasts who would simply not know if there was a problem with their car. This is another point, it is possible to be a classic car enthusiast and not know everything when it comes to maintaining a car. It is a learning process, after all, and some owners also simply have no interest in the mechanical side of things and just enjoy the polishing and the driving, which is absolutely fine as long as they hire someone else to ensure it is safe.

I also worry about press for the classic car community if an unroadworthy car is ever involved in a serious shunt, which is why even though the Magnette doesn't need to have a test, to make sure it is roadworthy I get Kel to thoroughly check it regularly and I ask him to be brutally honest with me. After all, he knows every nut and bolt on the car because he rebuilt most of it.

This being said, the majority of classic car owners know all this and are vigilant. It isn't just our own safety and the safety of our cars we worry about, but the safety of other road users too, but I really do think some kind of classic-friendly version of the MOT Test should be a requirement.

As my car hadn't been roadworthy since the early 1980s, it was also not registered as an historic vehicle, meaning that it was still listed as PLG and therefore liable to a charge. These days the charge is £210 a year, for a car registered before 2001 (as of April 2024). The process to get it changed to historic was easy though. All I had to do was take my V5C form to the post office and they did the work for me. I have known people to take forms to the post office and the clerk not know what to do, so I would recommend ringing ahead. I also took a Declaration of Exemption from MOT form — or V112 — but the clerk didn't seem to be concerned with that. He just tore off the relevant slip of my logbook and handed me a receipt for £0.00. We were taxed and insured. Technically, after 36 years the ZA was back on the road.

It felt really weird though. I had technically seen the project through. The car was registered, insured and essentially legal, but I didn't have it back yet. I'd called Sunny to let him know he could now test drive it legally, and there was a little stab of disappointment that I wasn't going to be the first person to drive it in 36 years — though I appreciated why it was best Sunny did it. I wouldn't know what I was looking for, whereas Sunny would have in mind a mental list of what to look out for.

But there wasn't much time to dwell on that, or even wonder when the car might be back. Our baby was due on September 7th, and as things stood we didn't know what was going to happen as they were currently the wrong way round. Everything was pretty normal, excluding Covid, throughout the whole pregnancy, other than one night at the end of July when things didn't seem quite right. Sophie and I had had a row and I'd gone for a walk, being mindful to take my phone with me because, after all, she was seven months pregnant and might need me, regardless of how much she wouldn't have wanted to see me at that point. For this reason, I also didn't walk very far, and I was glad of that when I got a phone call from a very upset Sophie to tell me she was scared because she couldn't feel the baby moving.

I've never run as fast.

When I flung myself through the door of the house, she was already putting her shoes on, and on the drive to Whiston I was doing my best to maintain calm and not pass any of my worry on to Sophie, who was already worrying enough, though internally I was in pieces. To make matters worse, once we got to hospital I wasn't allowed to go in with Sophie. I got as far as the double doors going into the ward before I was turned away. I was never angry or aggressive about it, though I thought the whole situation was bollocks. Covid policies were never the fault of the staff on the front line, and I was always very careful to keep my feelings private, as they would have been subject to enough grief without another dad having a go. I always thought that partners not being allowed to be together for antenatal appointments did more harm than Covid ever would, but I appreciate not everyone will agree and that it was uncharted territory at the time.

I also wasn't sure if Sophie had any signal or if she was allowed to use her phone, so once she went through those doors, I had no idea what was happening. Was she okay? Was she in labour? Was the baby okay? Was I a dad? All the questions started flooding in as I walked circuits of the hospital outside, calling my mum for some company, and also to keep her up-to-date on what was going on. I was on my own for a couple of hours, so I scouted where some nearby shops were and a takeaway in case today wasn't the day and I needed them when the time came. On this night I just bought a drink and walked back towards the hospital grounds in case I got a call to return quickly. It was dark but still quite warm as I looped around the car park for the millionth time, avoiding the smokers – I have since quit, and stayed quit – and taking the long way to the entrance, which was by now locked. I'd have to buzz if I needed to get in, and that only made me worry even more that it would delay any attempt to reach Sophie quickly. Then my phone buzzed with a WhatsApp, then it rang before I had a chance to open the message. Sophie.

She was ok, and more than a little relieved, and our baby was also okay. It had taken so long because once they'd established that the baby was fine they wanted to monitor them both. The WhatsApp was a recording. Knowing how much I'd worry, Sophie took a sound recording of the baby's heartbeat when they had the monitor on, and I'm glad she did. I only listen to it sometimes now that my son is here, but it's a nice thing to have and I have it in a file with photos of his scans. I had, by this point, started to try and hear the baby's heartbeat by gently pressing my ear against Sophie's bump and trying different places until I found it. I had read that you could hear the heartbeat in this way during the last few weeks of pregnancy and I can vouch that it works. The room has to be pretty quiet and there is definitely a knack to it, but we ended-up making a little routine of my listening for the baby's heart last thing at night after I'd put cream on Sophie's bump. It might be seen as a risky game for someone with anxiety as bad as mine — what if I didn't catch the heartbeat? — but once I'd sussed how to do it I can't remember too many times of me not being able to find it.

There was still plenty of room for worry though before our baby was due. Towards the end of August, we were in the car and Sophie turned to me and said: 'The baby's just done something really weird.'

Until that point, apart from the night when our baby was quiet and made us go to hospital in a panic (and cut a row short) things had been pretty straightforward if you remove Covid from the mix. It was a lovely summer and Sophie was stuck at home for most of it and by August she was ready to not be pregnant anymore, and we both just wanted our baby. But right at the end, literally a couple of weeks before our due date, Baby tried to throw a spanner in the works. At a check-up, it turned out that the 'really weird' thing they had done in the car was turn themselves around into the breech position. Sophie was told, while I sat in the car, that they would try what's called an ECV, or external cephalic version, which basically means someone tries to manipulate the baby back into the right position by putting pressure on the mum's bump. If that didn't work — they said — then they'd book Sophie in for a C-section.

It was a difficult situation to be put in, because we both wanted what was best for our baby, and I wanted what was best for Sophie, but we had also been spending months on a birth plan which we'd grown attached to. Sophie wanted to be in a midwife-led unit and give birth naturally, using Hypnobirthing techniques we learned from a woman in St Helens called Rachel Akehurst. She had to run the course over Zoom, but it was brilliant. It was all about positive affirmations and how mums can approach going into labour and how to deal with contractions, or 'surges' as she called them. She also taught dads how they could be supportive, and although I was definitely about as useful as a chocolate teapot, she made me feel helpful as I set about making a playlist for Sophie and listening to affirmations with her before bedtime each evening. I found them so relaxing I was normally asleep before Sophie was.

With this plan in place, Sophie found it frustrating to be told there was a good chance it wouldn't happen. Apparently ECVs so late into pregnancy rarely work, and one of the things they can do is bring on labour. To say I couldn't concentrate on my book about car number plates as I sat in the car park waiting for news was an understatement. The good news was, that for an ECV to be successful it's important the mum is relaxed going into the procedure, so Sophie had what we hoped would be a trial run for her hypnobirthing techniques. The good thing about visiting hospital frequently during August 2020 was abusing the 'Eat Out to Help Out' scheme at the Costa, and with Sophie's ECV being on a Wednesday, the last day of the week you could get the 50% discount deal on meals, I had bought myself plenty of food thanks to the Chancellor's — whom some of the papers called 'Rishi Two-Snacks' — deal. Not that I was feeling able to eat while I waited for Sophie. I may have piled weight on during the various states of lockdown thanks to countless trips to the fridge while being stuck at home, but the cheese and ham toastie and chicken ciabatta were sticking their smells to the car upholstery as I left them to cool, though anyone who has ever bought a cheese and ham toastie from Costa will know it never reached room temperature, it's still hotter than the Sun.

And then Sophie appeared. Still pregnant. And smiling.

'Done. It's worked. For now.'

That's another thing about an ECV. If they do work, baby can flip back again.

Relieved, I offered Sophie the cooling toastie and took the cold chicken ciabatta, not telling her I'd bought both for me and taking the credit for having thought of her.

The baby had to be monitored before and after the procedure, but other than that Sophie was back sitting next to me in the car long before I'd expected her. She told me the breathing techniques definitely helped. For now, tentatively, our original plan was back on. All we had to do was wait, and hope Baby didn't shift back into the breech position.

But due dates are strange really. No one knows for sure exactly when a baby is 'due'. They come when they're ready, and while it's nice to have a vague idea of when a baby is going to arrive, we made a point of not telling people when the date was. It's hard to believe people would ask: 'Has she had the baby yet?' — What do they expect me to say? 'Yeah, she had the baby last week but we just decided not to tell you.'

Due dates just put pressure on parents, so when ours came, we went to queue-up outside IKEA in Warrington to pass the time. We were in Sophie's Insignia, and it was raining in-between wiper speeds, which is one of the most annoying things in the world, one step above Audis, which don't indicate. And my phone rang as we were coming off the M6 and going up the slip road towards the utopia of flat pack, even if there were strict rules about how many shoppers were allowed in at a time. I honestly can't even remember what we were going for, though I can guess we left with tea lights and a plant.

My rule is to have my phone out of sight and out of mind in the car. I'd like to think I'd never be tempted to pick it up in traffic, but to be ultra sure I keep it in the boot. There's no point testing your self-control if you don't have to. I don't even like having it hooked-up via Bluetooth, but during Sophie's pregnancy I did just in case there was an emergency while I was out in her car. I could see from the screen that the call was from Sunny, and I managed to press the button on the steering wheel to answer the call without changing the radio station or setting a speed limiter to 14mph like I did once by accident in Edinburgh city centre and was convinced for a couple of minutes that the car was broken.

I was doing the 'I can't do two things at once' and speaking very slowly, with long pauses for traffic lights and roundabouts, perfectly demonstrating why all phone use other than calls to emergency services should be banned when driving. It was September 7th, a Monday, and early afternoon. When I saw that it was Quest phoning I honestly thought it would be to ask me to order more parts.

'Tom, your car is ready. You can pick it up.'

I punched the air and did a silent '*yeeaaah*'.

Every fibre of my body, except one, wanted to turn the car around, go home and get Maggie. The one that didn't was the one that wanted to take stock. I knew I would be nervous as hell the first time I drove it, and I wanted to do it on my own time, without rushing back from Warrington and without having curtailed one of the few times Sophie had left the house for more than a walk in six months (even if it was only to queue-up outside IKEA).

'We're just out at the moment, Sunny, I'm not sure when we'll be back. Can I ring later?'

It seemed anti-climatic. I'd been waiting my entire life for this moment and a trip to IKEA was holding me back.

There were a couple of spots of rain as we queued in the miles' long zig-zag to enter IKEA. I think queuing to get into shops during 2020, anxious that the people behind or in front of you might kill you, but also willing to endure it just to have something to do, was a glimpse into what purgatory must be like.

I flipped and flopped between wanting to get the car on the way home and wait until tomorrow.

I decided on the way back from IKEA that driving Maggie for the first time wasn't to be done in rush hour traffic, even though the drive home was three miles. There was an awkward right-hander out of Quest's car park straight into a queue for traffic lights and you can't see much of what's going on to the left, so you have to rely on being let into the queue on the right while inching out. As we got closer to home I called Sunny.

'What time are you going home?'

21

Car Fanatics Mark III?

Maxi Cosi Pebble car seat
Cost when new: £299.95
Group: 0—13kg; 0—15 months
Mounting type: ISOFIX

I asked if Sophie minded dropping me off at Quest to fetch my car home as soon as we'd got back from IKEA.

I'd been alive for 32 years and 341 days and seen this car run once. Never on a road. I'd never driven it. I was a little excited, relieved, and very scared.

'Do you want me to follow you home?'

The offer was kind, and wanted.

'No, I'll get chatting, you carry on and I'll see you at home.'

Part of me wanted to make sure Sophie didn't see me grapple with a car that scared me. And I would, and did, get chatting.

Seeing the car complete, and out in the open, was different to the times I'd seen it on my drive. Knowing it was a functioning, living car after so long made it look and feel more significant than when I'd previously seen it in daylight, and it looked tiny.

Sunny greeted me. I think, while he was evidently happy to see me drive the car home, he was a bit sad to see it go. For a business that usually dealt with much more financially valuable cars than mine, Maggie made an impression. Among cars worth literally hundreds of thousands of pounds, I don't think many would have meant as much to their owners. I'd definitely never have swapped.

We chatted, as I always do, and Sunny started the car for me. I climbed into the driver's seat behind the Magnette's running engine for the first time. The suspension springs hadn't lost their reassuring groan. It sounded the same as when I used to sit in the same seat as a child and pretend to drive it, despite everything underneath being new or rebuilt. Sunny told me to take my face mask off. I'd forgotten to remove it after speaking to him because of the emotions running through my body.

Then, as I thought might happen, my clutch foot started shaking. It was uncontrollable, worse than anything I had ever experienced as a learner driver with my dad sitting next to me.

I gave it a lot of gas as I eased that shaky left foot off the floor. I was expecting the clutch to feel heavy and had deliberately put on my most worn-in trainers to maintain as much control as possible. I clicked the handbrake and made a swipe for first gear, missed and went to grab it again. I was literally shaking. The gears grated slightly as a shuffled the lever into place. It sounded more like a drunk man trying to pass wind quietly than a crunch.

Before the big day, I'd been to Halfords to buy a fire extinguisher, tow rope and a stick-on rear-view mirror. I knew the one in the car was loose and wouldn't stay in place once it had been adjusted. I'd stuck the new one into place before setting off and made sure I had a full view of who would be driving up my arse. I'd driven an old car enough to know that some motorists had ample patience and some were too interested in what you were driving to pressure you. Others see old and know that equals slow. They either drive too closely behind you or overtake at unsafe moments.

There wouldn't be anything to worry about on that score. My plan to avoid traffic, even with a lot of people still working from home, was unsuccessful. The queue at the lights for my right hander out of the car park stretched as far as I could see, and those in it couldn't see my indicator, seeing as it was an illuminated orange stick behind my head. I didn't have to wait long to be waved out, and acting as if I was manoeuvring an artic lorry, I hauled the little car onto a public road for the first time, looking right the whole time in case someone sped around the corner and into the queue. I waved at the man behind me, put the car in neutral and stuck the handbrake on. Breathe.

For once, the lights changed quickly, I was up, I had to go. Shaky foot. The gears farted into place again and for the first time I had second, another little crunch. Then third, no crunch. Then a queue. Thank God. Rest those shakes.

When the traffic got moving again I was feeling better, I could feel the revs going up (though I couldn't see as the Z-types don't have a rev counter) and I began to ignore people looking at me and concentrate on my driving. Hell, I might even enjoy this, and as I got up to the heady heights of third gear and into the 20s on the speedo I was enjoying it. I wanted my dad to be there. I wished my dad was there. I decided to believe he was sitting in the passenger seat, whatever my brain and logic thought, I'd let my heart win today.

I'd sort of started to get used to the gearbox on the way up the gears. I knew what to expect with the steering (heavy at slow speeds is an understatement) and I knew what to expect with having drum brakes all round and planned accordingly (heavy, brake with plenty of planning, adjust speed with gears whenever possible). The hardest thing I was finding was changing down gears. They crunched every single time because I'd never driven anything older than a 1973 Triumph GT6 for a review in *Classic Car Weekly* and even that felt modern by comparison.

I've never really thought about driving, I've always just felt it instead, and I was catching myself thinking about what I was doing on this drive. It would come with practice I thought as I put the indicator on to turn into my road home. The indicator, I felt, would never cease to be a pleasing novelty.

Yes, I had been chatting, but I could tell Sophie was relieved to see me back in one piece. I was buzzing and I wanted my mum to see this. She had no idea the car was ready and I wanted to surprise her. I asked Sophie if she wanted a ride. If someone suggested taking a woman for a drive in a car built in 1956 when she is one day past her due date to me I would be amazed they'd even thought about it. I reasoned that my mum's house was only around the corner, and Sophie was up for it, and she's her own boss.

I started up Maggie, the car was still warm from the very short, but eventful, drive home and it went first time. We got to the end of our street and just about to go down the hill onto the main road and the Magnette coughed. Then it stuttered. Then it died.

I'd done three miles in total.

I pulled over to the side of the road, conscious I was blocking a driveway. The man whose house it was came outside, but it was to admire the car instead of tell me to move. The level of sympathy I received told me he had either been there or just understood. Thinking on my feet, I knew the fuel gauge was probably not working as it relies on a float attached to an arm to send a signal to the dash. It hadn't been asked to move in more than 30 years so was probably gummed-up. Maybe we were out of juice. Luckily, a petrol station was just around the corner, and if I jogged I could buy a can, fill it and be back in about 10 minutes, so off I went. Sophie stayed with the car, and the dog who was on the back seat.

Clearly, the lockdown stone had placed a new burden on my jogging ability, and even though the total run was less than a kilometre, I was puffing by the time I rounded the corner, extortionately-priced fuel can and petrol in hand, to top up the car. And it had started to rain. I told Sophie that I'd got it from here and she could go home. It's not like she had far to walk.

I consoled myself with the thought I needed the fuel can anyway as I poured it into the car to the satisfying slosh of an empty tank getting a much-needed drink, and I was sure by the sounds it was making that this was indeed the problem. The way the car gradually chugged and died also suggested to me that I was onto something. I jumped back in the driver's seat, tried it with the choke out this time, turned the ignition on, hit the starter button.

The starter motor whirred away. Nothing. Choke in. Try again. Nothing.

I phoned Sunny.

Sunny sounded as crestfallen as I was. I had tried to be objective and tell myself that breakdowns were going to happen, but I honestly expected to get more than three miles in on my first outing. I remember thinking, as I was waiting for Sunny to arrive, that the car shouldn't be out as the rain pattered on the windscreen, and I also thought how amazing the car smelled. I had smelled the mixture of leather, oil, petrol and wood a thousand times before, but it never didn't remind me of my dad, and it also reminded me of his dad now, as it is the smell of his garage. His house has long been sold and has since been completely remodelled, so it only exists in our memories now, but the car being in my garage has made that smell like his house. I don't have to wonder if he'd approve of the rescue effort on the car he bought for my dad's 27th birthday.

I heard Sunny arriving in the van before I saw him, and Kel was riding shotgun. Straight away they had the bonnet up and the pair of them started scouring for a fault, and although I was worried they hadn't found anything, I was also quietly pleased I hadn't missed anything bleedin' obvious. They decided to hook up the tow ropes to take the car back to Quest to find out what was wrong. I waved them off, trudged up the hill towards home and closed the garage door with a thud when I arrived. I'd briefly had my car back, but the garage would stay empty for at least another day.

It turned out to be a very simple problem to fix.

The starter motor and solenoid are connected by a spade connector (a flimsy wire, basically) and that was loose. Without a good connection, when the ignition button was pressed, not enough current was getting from the ignition to the starter motor, so it wouldn't start. It must have been knocked loose on the drive home, but it was now reconnected and secured with a few cable ties to stop it slipping. Replacing the wire at some point was probably a job to do.

My shaky clutch foot was nowhere near as bad as I pulled out of the Quest car park for a second time in as many days, and there was only one place I needed to go as the sunlight hit the wood and leather in the car, making it smell incredible.

I don't know how my mum knew I was on my way and I don't know how she knew which car I'd be in, but she was waiting on the front steps of her house as I rounded the corner, phone in hand to film Maggie pulling into the road where she spent her hibernation. I tooted the horn as I drove past and swung the car around at the top of the cul-de-sac, heaving the steering wheel as if I were trying to do a three-point turn in a boat.

I love the horn on that car, and thankfully my mum said the new horns sounded the same as she remembered. It's operated by a silver ring in the middle of the steering wheel and it sounds like an American school bus pulling onto the *Sesame Street* set.

Because of where the horn push is located, the fact it's very big, and also very sensitive, means it's very easy to push unintentionally as well.

Any sort of wiring job around the dashboard will result in being shocked out of your skin because of an unexpected blat of the horn, and if someone is simultaneously working under the bonnet, they'll crack their head on the bottom of the grille. My dad once told me it happened to him when my parents were cleaning the car for a show, and my mum pressed the horn while polishing the push, making my dad jump up from under the bonnet.

I could see memories like this through my mum's face. The car was a lot older, had been through some extensive surgery and still needed a few parts of the interior, such as door cards, putting back, but I was pleased she was finally looking at the car in a working state after all the help she'd given me (mostly financial and emotional support) since the car first went to Quest. It was my project, but the grief which started it belonged to all of us.

The timing had been perfect. We were still waiting for the arrival of our baby and I was just about to start working, just in time to start supporting a family. I'd been in my new job for a week and anxiously checking my phone at every opportunity in case there was news on the baby front.

It was a Monday, and I was teaching shorthand to a group in Manchester for the third time — I'd started the previous Thursday. I said to them if I look at my phone and run out the room, it's because my wife is in labour. A few smiled, but one or two looked genuinely concerned for me. I was new to teaching and hadn't mastered the art of being jokey with a classroom. Still haven't.

It was a beautiful day, when summer decides it's going to give you one of those last hurrahs in mid-September. Sophie was messaging me the usual stuff on my way home. The 'what time will you be home?' and the 'love you' were all normal as I boarded the train and buried my head into my book. Commuting at the time was bliss. Almost everyone was still working from home, so when the Northern Rail Pacers squeaked up to the platform with their sticky hot diesely scent you knew you were not just going to get a seat, but a whole carriage to yourself. It was the complete opposite of the same journeys back when I was teaching before Boris Johnson had told pregnant women to stay at home. Back then you had to squeeze on and pray you'd be able to see out the window enough for when it was your stop.

I got off at Orrell, where, if you were lucky enough to be on a new train with toilets, you had to work out via a complicated formula which carriage you need to be on to be able to get off at the short platform.

'If you're on a carriage which has a toilet but you are at the back of the train, please move to one without a toilet, unless you are at the front of the train then you'll want one with a toilet.'

This game had caught me out the week before, and the doors between the carriages were locked, meaning I was on until the next stop at Upholland. I feel guilty to this day, but it's the one time I've ever given a member of staff on public transport a hard time, and it wasn't their fault. Train staff, service industry staff and shop workers seem to be the ones most in the line of fire.

On this particular Monday there were no issues — I'd got the right carriage and was able to take the Moon landing-style leap from the train onto the platform below before taking the stairs two at a time to go and look for Sophie, who had insisted on saving me the 20 minutes' walk home so she could pick me up in the car.

She had sunglasses on and looked beautiful.

I opened the car door and smiled to myself as I looked at the seatbelt cradling her bump and how amazing I thought she was for insisting she drove while a week overdue with our baby.

'I don't want you to get excited,' she started as I lowered myself into the car and decided where to put my feet as my backpack took space in the footwell. 'But. I've been having contractions since 11 o'clock this morning.'

Not only was she very likely in labour, but she was driving me home. All I can remember of getting home was that Sophie was trying to calm me down and as I brought her pilates ball into the lounge I was wondering when to take her to hospital. The time came when the contractions were, what felt like to me, nanoseconds apart and accompanied with expressions from Sophie which told me she was very uncomfortable. I didn't do the Colin McRae impression on the way to Whiston, a drive you can do in under half an hour from Billinge in normal conditions and I did my best to be calm. I tried to drive normally, and when we got to hospital and I negotiated the ramps in the car park and found a space without issue, I assumed we were good for the night. It was a little past eight by this point.

Sophie was still able to walk and a few people gave us knowing nods and the odd smile as we weaved our way to the ward, with Sophie clutching her bump and me trying to be supportive but getting in the way. We both had bags packed, but I'd left them in the car in case we didn't need them, and we reasoned it would be easier to deal with the bags when I was able to run, rather than be in place to try to help but really get in the way of a woman having a baby.

We arrived at the ward and Sophie went in.

I wasn't allowed in because of the risk of spreading Covid, so I sat on a low windowsill with a long line of other dads, putting us all in closer proximity with one another than we otherwise would have been. It was like a queue at a deli counter but without the raffle tickets. Occasionally a nurse or midwife would pop their head out of the door and call one of us in. The rest of us would look at each other and then back down at the floor. None of us had any phone signal.

What felt like ages passed — it was dark outside — and instead of a nurse calling me in, Sophie walked out and told me to go with. I was confused.

We were going home, she told me. This made me panic.

'What's up, have they told us to go? Will it be a long time?'

We had been sent home, for the time being, and told to call back when things looked like they were moving along. I was still pretty terrified, thinking the hospital is where I wanted everyone to be. But we headed for the car, with me thinking at least I could just turn around and come back. So we got in the car and headed for home at around 9.00pm.

Something wasn't right.

There are lots of windy country roads between Whiston Hospital and home and I was constantly being told to slow down by Sophie, more uncomfortable by the second. At one point a very angry driver who had been flashing his lights at me for a while overtook and I can't blame them. They didn't knowmy passenger was a woman in labour and I was doing 17mph in a 60 zone! As I eventually managed to wind the car back towards Billinge, over the beautiful and now dark countryside, I heard a groan.

'My waters have just broken.'

I hit the contacts button on the screen and called 'Maternity Triage' (it's still saved in my phone) and was glad I'd set the hands free up.

As I turned the car around the phone was answered pretty quickly.

'You've just sent my wife home and her waters have broken in the car, so we're coming back.'

I asked Sophie if she minded me driving a little quicker than 17mph as I didn't fancy delivering our baby in her car, though that would have been a fantastic way to end a car book.

So we went, at a nearly normal speed, stopping once for her to be sick. I was extra careful on the ramps at the car park. By this time it was quiet, and I was able to park right next to the entrance, which was over a walkway suspended over the main road and into the building. As we parked, I raced around the car and opened Sophie's door. She couldn't get out. She was unable to walk as her contractions, sorry — surges — were happening what felt like every two seconds and I was starting to get scared. We were so close to being in the right place but also oh-so-close to having a baby in the car park. A couple walked past the car as Sophie let out a loud moan and instinctively shushed her. You know when something comes out of your mouth and you immediately regret it? I still cringe at having done it, when I think about it I go a bit weak because it was a gross thing to do.

The couple were about level with the back of our car.

'DON'T FUCKING SHUSH ME.'

That was me told.

I ran to find a wheelchair, convinced I'd return to find a baby on its way out. It was early autumn-evening chilly and the height of the walkway was making the breeze seem stiff. The walkway at night haunted me. The metal mesh sides let a very light flurry of snow through the gaps on the night my dad died and I thought of him every time we came here. Whiston had the midwife-led unit Sophie so wanted to use and it shouldn't even have been a consideration if I was ok with it. I joked, because my dad and his parents all died here that Whiston was where McCooeys went to die. I wanted to banish that.

It felt like I was in a video game. Find the wheelchair before your wife gives birth in the car park and get her to the right place in the hospital. You lose points for every time you crash the wheelchair into the wall or go too fast over a bump. There was a cluster of wheelchairs just inside the automatic doors, the old type with leatherette covers and all the wheels are the same size. The fuckers are impossible to steer. It would have to do. I ran back to the car.

It felt like an age between the car and the delivery suite. You have to go into the hospital from the car park, down the lift, past what were by now closed Costa and WH Smith stores and back up another lift. By ten past 11, I was back in the queue of dads sitting on the windowsill. I wasn't on the windowsill for long.

'Mr McCooey?'

I looked up.

'Come on, dad. It's your turn.'

The staff couldn't have been nicer as I walked through into the suite, which was exactly what Sophie wanted. What I didn't want was the sight of a large poster as I walked through the corridor informing me that one in every 200 births end in stillbirth. That is, when a baby dies before they are born after 24 completed weeks of pregnancy. It's a figure that seems unacceptably high to me, but I'm not an expert and I'm sure people cleverer than I am are doing a lot to bring it down. I don't know how people who go through it manage.

What a horrendous thought to be going into the delivery suite with. Nice one. I tried to shake it out of my head as I went through to Sophie.

The birthing pool was being filled in the frankly huge room, which also had a shower and a bed, while Sophie sat in a chair. She was offered gas and air, but after a quick go she told me it wasn't doing anything, so she went without. By 11.30, she was in the water and looked much more comfortable. The lights were low, the playlist I'd spent months agonising over was on and Sophie's cork board of affirmations and pictures to make her feel calm was on display in a corner, not being looked at. And, again, the staff couldn't have been more amazing. They sensed Sophie just wanted to get on with it so they let her.

When the midwife told us Sophie didn't have to wait long, she wasn't lying. She was checking with a mirror and she asked Sophie if she minded if dad had a look. I didn't want to look. I just wanted my wife and baby to be ok, and I was happy trickling water on Sophie's shoulders as she breathed through each contraction and made it look easy. I bet it wasn't, but as I react to stubbing my toe like I've been shot, I think Sophie was enjoying proving a point.

My mental state robbed me of joy for the first few seconds of William's life.

He was born at exactly 1.30am on 15th September and 'Breezeblocks' by alt-J was playing, which was lovely as some of the lyrics give a nod to my favourite children's book, *Where the Wild Things Are*.

Sophie lifted him and told me: 'You have a boy.' I'll never forget that.

But I'll also struggle to forget that William was silent for what was probably three seconds but felt like three minutes. The midwife didn't take him off Sophie but placed a hand behind his back and prodded his chest a few times sharply with two fingers. I think she was just about to start getting worried, maybe, when he let out a cry. It was the most relieved I have ever been.

After all the Covid restrictions, I was never asked to leave, and when morning rolled around and Costa opened I was allowed to procure baked goods for my wife and return. I have spoken to some dads that were given 30 minutes post birth with their partners and babies. We were in the hospital together for more than 11 hours. They pretty much left us to it, allowed us to take our time, have cuddles, showers and make sure we were right before we headed towards home via the most important drive of my life.

22

Two-Brew Job

1976 MG Midget 1500
Another Midget that means a lot to me belongs to my
mate, Gary Brunskill, who is my go-to home mechanic
and life guru. Gary says he wouldn't have bought his
Midget without my influence, but he influences me
much more than I do him.

We rotated in a shift pattern in the early days, so we each got some sleep. There wasn't much driving of my newly-restored car to be done, even when I was told, repeatedly by people around me, to do things for myself. I was too mindful of wanting to do enough with William and for Sophie.

I did go out for the odd drive, but I felt guilty. I would come home smelling of old car and feel like I needed to have a shower and change my clothes before being with our baby, and I was also worried about nipping out for half an hour and then being stuck for hours with a broken down car. Drives were laps of the village and no further, for that reason.

Sophie and I tried to do three hours on, three hours off, in the first few weeks and it worked well with a newborn. It didn't always quite work out that way as Sophie needed to feed him, and I couldn't do that unless we had some in a bottle, which isn't always straightforward.

I was able to give him bottles of breastmilk from time to time, and the sitting up at night wasn't really an issue with a newborn, you can just cuddle them and watch the telly. Apart from the lack of sleep, there are many aspects of having a toddler which are much harder. Le Mans was on over the first weekend of his life, so I was more than happy to do the night shift.

When I did think about Maggie, there was enough still to do to keep me occupied on the occasions I did get out to the garage and I'd already started gathering bits on my list.

Requiring immediate attention was a temperature gauge which didn't work, so Peter Martin supplied me with a new, specially-made temperature sender unit. At £80 it wasn't cheap for a piece of metal about the size of my little finger (and I have very small hands) but they don't make little bits like this for cars approaching their mid-60s anymore and these were made to order in America.

Also on the list was a day to look at the dynamo, which appeared not to be charging the battery as the ignition light remained on when the car was started. The handbook said it should go off shortly after starting, and if the car was driving just on the battery, that would drain over anything approaching middle distance. To be sure I wouldn't get caught out on my drives around the village, the car remained on near-permanent trickle charge when it was home.

The fuel gauge also needed sorting. It definitely wasn't working, as a fresh glug of £20's worth of petrol confirmed, and by now there was too much fuel to fix the problem, as taking the sender unit out of the tank would reveal a big hole from which new petrol would pour out all over me and the car boot. I needed to do some driving before attending to that, then.

I also needed to put back my map pocket and other bits of

trim, as well as look for a new door card for the driver's door, or a way to spruce up the one I had.

For us and William, our time as a new family was quiet. The day before he was born, the 'rule of six' banning gatherings of more than six people came into force, so our contact was with close family only, and a couple of weeks later when my car's new logbook had arrived showing 'historic' under the vehicle category, the tier system was brought in. Greater Manchester was placed in the top tier (or was it bottom?), meaning we were effectively locked down again, and Merseyside, which we can see when we look out our upstairs window, was in the more relaxed Tier Two. It didn't feel fair at all.

My logbook had arrived on October 3rd, the day after my birthday, which was spent in a nice restaurant while I had a beer and cuddled my new son in-between Sophie feeding him and trying to manage her own food. You were allowed beer with food, apparently eating reduces the risk of catching covid. Rumours about another lockdown were doing the rounds and we reasoned that the restaurants we loved, however tight our own financial situation was, may not be there anymore when we came out the other side, so we went for it. A month later, the second national lockdown was confirmed. The three of us, and Otis, were in for a cosy winter.

There wasn't much I could do with the MG over winter except for starting it to make sure everything was ticking over and still working. I moved it up and down the drive to stop the tyres flat spotting and to make sure the brakes had some use, but I wasn't keen on even doing an 'essential' journey to the shops in it in case I had a problem and had to justify why a vehicle which was clearly intended for pleasure was out when we were all supposed to be inside.

I couldn't see Gary to help me out with a lot of the jobs I wanted to do, and there wasn't much point anyway as I couldn't go out in the car to enjoy my handiwork. There was one afternoon the day after lockdown was announced that I cleaned up some bits of trim that I knew I needed to refit, but I couldn't find a way to get the map pocket back into place without bending it, and I didn't want to cause any damage so I left it alone. I decided, instead, to look at this lockdown as a chance to spend some time with my wife and son. The car would still be in the garage when it was over.

William's first Christmas came and went, with a chance to see some family on Christmas Day as we thankfully avoided being placed into the dreaded 'Christmas is cancelled' Tier Four, but we were, sure as night follows day, back in a lockdown on January 6th, a year and three days after we found out we were having William.

With such little opportunity to do any meaningful driving, it was inevitable that as soon as I did venture off the drive there would be a problem. Conscious of the fact the car had moved only up and down the drive for weeks on end, I decided it was coming with me to the shops one cold, but dry, afternoon in February, 2021. All seemed ok. It started on the button and I wasn't bothered by the cold as I slammed the door shut and took in the view. The huge bakelite steering wheel felt thin and old-fashioned. I was no longer nervous about driving it, and I was looking forward to a drive I was going to enjoy, however short, like I enjoyed driving my Midget. Once off the housing estate and onto the main road, I felt a shudder. I immediately thought I must be doing something wrong. I carefully dipped the clutch, found second without crunching (too much) and pressed the throttle. All seemed well again — I assumed my lack of driving had caused some fuel to go stale or maybe a bit of grot was finding its way through the system. Back into third, throttle, shudder.

Clearly, something wasn't right. I knew I could nurse the car home in second, so before I threw a tantrum and cursed my awful luck, I decided to get home safely and do the 'fuck my life' routine later. I eased the car into the garage and stepped out to find a trail of liquid, about the width of a line had it been drawn with a ballpoint pen, coming all the way up the road and following my car into the garage. I hunched down on my hands and knees, feeling the cold as I pressed my nose towards tarmac to have a smell. Petrol.

Once you've decided which liquid is coming from a leak, the next thing you need to do is find out where from. I opened the bonnet and ducked my head under the huge front grille to see if I could make sense of what was going on. There was no sign of anything, and no puddle under the car for that matter, so I fired it up to see if that would do anything.

Sure enough, from one of the carburettors came a cascade of petrol resembling a chocolate fountain in a shopping arcade, only it would definitely be best not to eat the contents spewing from here. I switched off and wondered, with my limited car knowledge, what to do. I had a novel idea, I was going to read the handbook and have a bit of a Google instead of blindly wielding a spanner in fading light.

After reading I hoped to find, when I did open up the carburettor float chamber, a brass float at the bottom of the pot instead of floating at the top. The idea is that as petrol pours into the float chamber from the fuel pump, a brass float pushes the top of the chamber when it is full and shuts off a switch. If the float no longer does its job, it doesn't rise to the top, the switch doesn't shut off and petrol continues to pour into the float chamber and out of the sides.

Being brave, for me, I took a socket wrench to the top of one of the float chambers, after carefully deciding which size was best by doing a test with my untidy box of loose sockets, and I started off gently, before gradually increasing the force needed until I felt the nut budge. The smell of petrol took my mind off the sharp February chill in the garage and I found exactly what I was hoping for, a chamber full of fuel and a brass float stuck to the bottom. In instances like this I really should take more precautions, such as wearing gloves, but I immediately prodded my right index finger into the chamber to see if I could bounce the float out of the chamber to inspect it. All that achieved was splashing a small amount of fuel into the immediate vicinity, so instead I went with the longest flathead screwdriver I could find and I fished it out. Sure enough, there was a tiny crack in the brass float, which I was now holding in a piece of petrol-y kitchen towel. Taking a picture on my phone, the next step was for me to get back in touch with Peter Martin. I left the carb float on the floor of the garage but still dragged the petrol smell in with me — it sticks to your clothes like cigarette smoke and to your hands like garlic. Peter had what I needed for £28 each.

I had a choice to make. Did I want to order like for like, and get a brass part from someone else, or get what Peter had in stock, called a 'stay-up' float made from plastic. These wouldn't crack after exposure to modern petrol like the brass ones had, though they aren't original. Ethanol and brass don't like each other, apparently.

While I like originality, I also think it should only go so far. My approach to most situations is that if the car had been on the road for the entirety of its life, with one owner who didn't cherish it as a classic, but used it as a car, what improvements would they make? It's clearly not applied to everything, as I am yet to fit seatbelts, flashing indicators or disc brakes to the car, all clear candidates, but when making certain decisions I will use the principle as a guide. In this case, you can't even see the part while it's doing its job, and I didn't want to get stuck in the same boat further down the line. I asked Peter for two 'stay-ups'. While I was replacing the broken brass float, I reasoned I may as well change the working one before it also broke.

I used a Saturday morning in early March to get the job done, fishing the remaining brass float out, dropping in the new ones (which bobbed around nicely when dropped into place) and tightened everything back up with a satisfying click of my socket spanner which emitted sounds of 'person who lives here knows what they're doing' tones. I started-up and the lovely sound of the engine firing into life was not accompanied by gushing liquid and an over-working fuel pump. I jumped out, got onto my belly and looked under the car. No leaks. I felt useful.

On the Monday, I took advantage of working from home to use my daylight hours to tackle the non-functioning fuel gauge, and that meant another few hours in the boot.

Magnette boots are dark and cramped spaces I have become acquainted with, and despite the light outside, it still required the delicate balancing of a phone torch and I banged my head many times in the usual spot.

Helpfully, the fuel gauge sender unit is easy to get at. It is basically a thin metal arm with a barrel on the end of it. The barrel floats in the tank and raises the arm, which sends a signal to the gauge — '50s technology is gloriously simple and also ingenious.

The sender unit is behind some soundproofing and there are a few screws to undo before very carefully guiding the arm out of the tank — it's easy to bend and doing that would give you an inaccurate reading — not that these things are to-the-mile accurate anyway.

The stubbornness of the screws suggested I was the first person to access the tank in this way in a very long time, and with each loosening screw, the waft of petrol fumes told me we were getting closer until what we suspected was revealed — a very gummed-up sender. There is a hinge to allow the arm to move, and it had basically become stuck with years' worth of crap, made worse by the decades' of inactivity.

A very brittle gasket had to be sacrificed, so I needed to remember not to fill up more than halfway until I'd ordered one, but the good news was I was able to remove the sender, give it a decent wipe with some kitchen towel and then give it a more thorough clean until it started pivoting freely once again.

To my surprise, once I'd put everything back and banged my

head again, the gauge worked, so it was on to the temperature unit, which was a two-brew job with Gary the following day.

This is behind the radiator on the main block of the engine and access is a bit tight, but after some gentle persuasion the old unit came away with enough speed for me to whack my hand on something hard and metal and cut it. Add to this my laziness at not draining the coolant first, I had to act quickly to plug the hole with my finger before swapping said finger for the new sender unit while trying to lose as little coolant as possible — resulting in wet feet from coolant seeping through my canvas trainers. Topping up what was lost, after reconnecting relevant wires, I excitedly jumped back in the driver's seat to perform a test. Still no gauge.

I decided to have a poke around under the dash and, after some more contorting and mild swearing, found a loose wire and a hole the same width as said wire. I was unable to reach where this wire went with my stubby fingers, but Gary took my place and shoved the two together and — presto — the gauge moved across to 'cold' for the first time in God-knows how long. Could I have saved £80? Possibly, but the old sender unit looked pretty shot and Peter told me it was virtually certain to be broken anyway so fitting a new one was a good idea — perhaps just not in the hap-hazard way I chose to fit mine. I was building my confidence with each day spent in the garage with Gary. We'd usually stop and do a pie shop run at lunch and he'd always bring a *Wigan Observer* so I could see how the paper was doing now I no longer worked there. We just needed to get to the bottom of another issue — the one of the battery not charging. And there was another feeling nagging away at me with each announcement on Covid restrictions.

At the time I was teaching media law to students in London. The arrangement was I would travel down and stay over for a couple of nights a week, teaching in person for three days and teaching remotely or doing admin for the other two. As much as

I hated the idea of leaving my young family for a couple of nights a week, financially the job was an improvement on teaching shorthand in Manchester and I wanted to teach other subjects. The arrangement was temporary, with a move back to Manchester written into my agreement for the following September, and I figured it was worth the sacrifice. Still, working from home suited me just fine — the idea of leaving my young son for any length of time filled me with dread.

That intensified on March 8th, 2021, when it was announced education establishments could go back to work. I knew that one day I'd have to go, but every week spent at home was another week closer to August when working away was no longer on the table. I got a little stay of execution, as we waited until Step 2 of the so-called roadmap out of restrictions, when pupils on practical courses were allowed back on April 12th. My gig was to be at home on Mondays and Fridays, so my first train down to London was on Tuesday, April 13th.

There were tears. From me, not my seven-month-old son.

In the end it wasn't too bad. There was a lot of guilt in leaving Sophie with William, especially as our son wasn't, and still isn't, the best sleeper on the planet, meaning he's an appalling sleeper just like his dad. But by June I was down to one night per week instead of two as teaching loads had wound down. There were also a couple of weeks in the summer when Greater Manchester was labelled as a 'high risk' Covid area, and my employer decided it wouldn't look great to ship me into London from the petri dish to breathe my northern Covid germs all over a room full of students — so I was back on Zoom for a bit, and at home more often to take the car out for lunchtime drives.

One source of guilt for me is always the fact my mum's Midget spends so long in her garage between drives. My mum dutifully books it in for servicing every year, even though it rarely does more than 100 miles between checks, and she will start the car on a regular basis when she isn't driving it. It's literally around the corner from me, and I really should take it out more often. With fewer than 30,000 miles on the clock (just) it's a weird feeling to drive an old car that feels much newer. But at over 40 years old, there have been a few small cosmetic blemishes to attend to. The car has been garaged for all of its life, so doesn't have the usual telltale rust areas of a British Leyland car, or any dings from shopping trolleys or wayward footballs, but the driver's door was sufficiently tatty for me to sort out a replacement in July 2021 and ask Quest (who else, by this point) to fit it.

The door itself came from the MG Owners' club for £220, but my lack of skills meant the test fit, alterations, drilling for the door handle and mirrors, priming, colour matching, painting and fitting meant my mum had to find £1,500 — though it really did finish off the car, which is now pretty much perfect apart from a missing letter D where it is supposed to say 'MIDGET' on the passenger side sill. Luckily, I have a spare bag of Midget letters in my garage from a time when I was cleaning out some of my dad's stuff and decided to keep it for spares. Whereas I want my car to wear its age, my mum's is in such good condition, it seems appropriate to keep it as near to perfect as possible, though I don't think it would ever qualify as concours because some parts — such as the door and one of the front wings — aren't original.

With teaching in London winding down, and the end of my trips and a move to the company's Manchester office in sight, I had a renewed sense of optimism and confidence, using the available light in the evenings to get to the bottom of the niggles that were keeping me from driving any distance — mainly the charging issue.

Gary was kind enough to bring a mate, who is also an auto electrician, to one of our brews on the drive mornings in August. Paul Stephen is in his 70s and doesn't have to work, but recognises he's probably one of the only people left with sufficient knowledge of certain aspects of classic cars to keep them going. Those who should know, like me, either don't have the patience to learn or use time as an excuse and rely on others to keep their cars going. I fall into both of these camps.

I was convinced the battery wasn't charging because the ignition light was staying on once the engine had been started, and I was convinced that was because of the dynamo. Paul spread out his tools and stuck his head under the bonnet, and told me the dynamo was working fine. We'd tried a trick called 'polarising' the dynamo before, which needs doing when the battery is disconnected. This involves running a wire from the unearthed terminal on the battery and brushing it against what is known as the 'f' terminal a few times until it causes a small spark. It's sometimes called 'flashing the dynamo.'

I honestly can't say if this worked, or if there was a problem in the first place, but Paul decided the problem with my car was the voltage regulator box, which sits behind the engine, mounted to the car on two screws and basically ensures the voltage running to different parts of the car is correct through a series of coils. It's more complicated than that, but it would take up a whole chapter of its own and I'd bet anyone reading this would either not be bothered, already know, or have access to Google. Mine was ancient. I knew that because I hadn't bought one, and a replacement was probably best anyway. Cue Peter Martin, who had them in for £35.

I love getting parcels from Peter. It's not as if these are presents, I do swap the contents for money, but I delight in taking a pair of splayed scissors and running the blade along the brown tape to get into the box of parts. He sends the type of parcels that are impossible to get into as there is so much tape around the edges of the carefully-wrapped brown paper, but this is a demonstration that the stuff he is sending is well-looked after. It's always wrapped with enough newspaper to keep a china doll from breaking if it were sent through airport baggage handling and the hand-written invoices he has sent have gone straight in the car's history file, which has increased tenfold with receipts since I started the project. My scrawl of 'Paid' followed by whatever date I transferred funds to Peter has spoiled them — but I also hope one day it might be another dimension to the records kept about the car.

Fitting the regulator box was no bother. I did it on a Gary day and we designated it as a two-brew job. With anything where wires go in, you need to take advantage of modern technology and take a picture of the one that is in place before you take anything off. It's quicker than referring to a manual and, I think at least, it leaves less room for error if you're not nailed-on sure of what you're doing. I also think you're not going to learn anything if you don't try. Most of the time, the worst that is going to happen is something you try won't work, until you do it and it does, or you ask someone who knows. The times when I won't take that approach is when it's something that would affect safety for other people, such as brakes.

The box was easy to fit to the car — it was held on by two screws — but we had to be careful to take each of the five wires going into it out one by one, wrapping labelled tape around each one and photographing it to get the order right. The hardest part was making sure the wires stayed put when I tried to screw each one into place — they were short and very wide for the spaces I was trying to cram them into, but after a few head bangs, dropped screwdrivers and choice words, I was confident we'd got it right.

So with that sorted, and with a couple of months' of good weather, I'd be driving the crap out of the car, right?

Wrong.

I was appallingly bad at taking the car out, even for short jaunts to the shops. With William approaching his first birthday, I still felt like time spent on Maggie at weekends was time I could have been spending with him, and if there was a need to go out for even a short distance, getting the MG out necessitated moving two cars off the drive and finding somewhere to street park those to get it out of the garage. It just seemed to be a faff. Time slipped away, with a functioning car in the garage, I thought I'd do enough to keep it ticking over as other things took precedence.

William walked properly for the first time on August 26th 2021, a few weeks before his first birthday. He was already doing the odd step, and I was filming him when he took eight consecutive steps towards me — so I decided that was the moment we'd say he'd officially walked.

My work move to the Manchester office was also happening, meaning I was much happier, but much worse off for time and money. I was actually home less, because I was now in the office every day, rather than three days a week, and I was now paying for my transport, as my London trips had been covered as part of my arrangement.

I couldn't afford to drive to, and park in, Manchester, so I got the train which was near enough two hours door to door when you took into account a 20-minute walk either side of the train journey. Add to that the fact that Northern cancelled around a train a week, and sometimes by the time I got home, William would either be going to bed or already be in bed. And if he wasn't, I was going to spend those minutes of daylight with him instead of the car. But I was home every evening, and that made a big difference.

I finally had my graduation ceremony on William's first birthday, too. Post Covid, when I first left university I wasn't convinced it had been the right thing to do, and by this point I still wasn't. I had walked away with a distinction, undoubtedly because I had been a working journalist for most of my working life by the time I studied, and after a year of paying to live through inheritance, and spending money on the car, I felt I would have been better off staying at the paper, especially as my course was disrupted by Covid, and by the time I had a baby to provide for newsrooms were still not allowing new people into their organisations. I honestly think the pandemic, in many respects, altered my career path because I needed work so urgently in

September 2020. I loved the job I was in, because I love teaching, and I was no longer just teaching shorthand, but across pretty much the whole journalism spectrum from law to editing content. But my salary was lower than when I left the paper two years previously. As much as I enjoyed my job, I couldn't help but think I could have saved tens of thousands of pounds and also be working from home at this point, spending much more time with my son.

I did get some freelance broadcast work, including at BBC Radio Lancashire, but that wasn't the same as my aspirations to move my career into working in radio full-time.

It got as late as December when I finally decided to start Maggie. After a night leaving the battery on to charge, I turned the key to the satisfying clicking and chugging sounds of the fuel pump, and I hit the starter button. There was no whirring, willing the car into life. Just a click. Click.

I tried again. Click. Click.

One more time. Nothing.

It's so true that old cars really don't like not being used.

I should know, from my experience of being in a band, that when something doesn't work you go for the simplest solution first and work your way up until you've fixed the problem. If a light doesn't work, you replace the bulb before you go ripping wires out of the wall. If a guitar doesn't make a sound when strummed, you check that it's turned up, and then you look at the lead before you open up the amplifier and go at it with a soldering iron.

But of course, in my head, when the starter motor doesn't engage, it must mean that it's knackered. A starter motor is a fairly chunky piece of kit and costs about £100. I emailed Peter Martin again, who must have been getting sick of me.

His reply: "I very much doubt that you have killed the starter motor – they are usually very robust units. I think it's much more likely that you've a poor electrical connection somewhere in the system. Personally, I would try cleaning up the starter solenoid connections, and the starter motor lead connection."

So that's what I did.

On the 16th December, I know from my emails to Peter that the car was turning over — so it wasn't the starter motor after all, but it wouldn't fire-up until Gary arrived a day later. We gave the car a good once over, cleaning the spark plugs, and swapping out my starter coil for one Gary had brought because it allowed us to change the connection on the leads from the distributor cap. They were what is known as a push-in connector, and predictably don't offer as much stability as a screw-in connector as they loosen up more easily. After a lot of persuasion, and a little squirt of a starting aid we were running. The starting aid is essentially fuel that comes in an aerosol can and you squirt it into the air intake of the engine to encourage it to go. A few people will tell you that using these methods to start a car can damage an engine and cars can become 'addicted' to being started in this way. This is despite the claims from those who make the stuff that it causes no damage, so I was mindful, but desperate. It worked, though, and we were back up and running just in time for Christmas.

23

On With the Show

Little Tykes Cozy Coupe
Cost when new: £49.99
Cost of ours: £0
Top speed: 6mph when I'm pushing.

We were desperately looking forward to a Christmas without worrying about which of us would be 'locked down' for the day, with family arriving from as far as 200 miles away and as close as half a mile.

Including children we would be hosting 13 people in 2021 and as I take the role of chief meat cook, I couldn't wait. Sod presents, as much as I love seeing people open them, bleary-eyed and already full of chocolate on Christmas morning, if I had to keep one thing it would be being able to cook the turkey. Not everyone in our family would choose turkey, but my foot is down. Nothing fills the house in the same way as a turkey cooking at 8.00am and nothing else smells like Christmas Day nearly as much. When we were kids, our family always operated a free-for-all approach to Christmas presents. I still get too excited to sleep on Christmas Eve now, so you can imagine what I was like when I was a kid. I'd be wide awake all night and even wider awake by 6.00am. Mum would tell us we had to wait until seven so I'd literally watch the seconds tick by on the clock in the top corner of my portable telly screen on Ceefax. Bang on seven, I'd be in my parents' room with my brother and sister (in the days before my little brother was born).

My son was much too young to share in this excitement in 2020. I rocked him to sleep as I watched the Christmas Eve night service and in 2021, though he had a sleep routine, he was still in bed late as he's never been a great sleeper, and I had only just learned to chill out about it as we approached his third Christmas a year after that.

At 15 months old, he didn't know why there was a tree in the house (brought home by my trusty Insignia) or why his dad was getting excited about wrapping presents and collecting veg boxes and queuing at the butcher, but he seemed quite happy with the toy car and chocolate coins when he decided to wake up at 6.30 — like father, like son.

Our 13 became eight, though, as two of Sophie's sisters stayed at home with their partners thanks to Covid and my older brother was ill with a non-Covid-related ailment. It's a good job I bought some pastry for a Boxing Day pie.

There used to be a new Year's Day car meet at a pub called the Cornerhouse in Wrightingon, Lancashire, and having attended the last couple to cover for *Classic Car Weekly*, I was determined to see in 2022 by taking Maggie and making the most of the hangover-free mornings parenthood affords. It would also be the first show since being back on the road. Having not driven any great distance for so long, though, we needed a day of tinkering to make sure the car was up for the 20-mile round trip. A couple of days before, Gary was back for a day of playing cars and drinking brews.

The car started without any issues, thanks to the work we had done the week before, so we nipped to the petrol station for a splash of fuel and then did some serious driving to make sure there were no gremlins and to get everything primed for the drive to the show. The weather was perfect. It was cold but dry and sunny, and I couldn't help but beam with joy at doing the most miles in one go I'd ever done in the Magnette. It was finally starting to feel like my car as my confidence grew, and as the engine warmed and I glanced at the temperature gauge I'd fixed and saw it had sprung into life, I felt the car settle and run more smoothly. We stopped at the top of Shaley Brow in Billinge, near the beacon which means so much to me, for a picture of the car 'in the wild' and as we headed home, our thoughts turned to the event in a couple of days' time. It was only a small meet of about 50 cars or so, but the atmosphere was always great and I wanted to be a genuine part of the convoy of cars which would emerge a couple of miles out from the pub. I couldn't wait. The low sun was making me squint, I was cold, but happy. Winter drives like this are every bit as good as the summer ones.

As I pulled the car into my drive, I stopped and left it on the drive. We'd go inside for another cup of tea before putting it back in the garage.

I was in the kitchen, looking out at the darkening sky and I heard Gary fire-up the car. He likes to look under the bonnet with the engine running, and then tell me how good a job they did of rebuilding it. I finished washing my mug and went out to join him. As a matter of habit, I jumped down onto my stomach to take a look underneath. I'm obsessed with leaks, which is funny considering I have a 60-odd-year-old British car, but this time I saw something I really could have done without.

There was a puddle's worth of oil where tarmac should be, right under the driver's side. Corner House in the passenger seat of Gary's Midget it was, then.

Luckily the leaking stopped when we shut the engine off, so after wheeling the Magnette into the garage, condemning me to weeks' of headscratching in the process, I set to work with the

Fairy Liquid and a yard brush. You can tell which house is mine because of the oil stains on the drive, a feature I'm sure not many estate agents would be keen to promote. I also didn't want to piss the neighbours off.

I took a familiar seat next to Gary on New Year's Day, this time without a raging hangover and with a one-year-old asleep with his mum, rather than suspecting he was there but not officially knowing yet. And I was going in someone else's car. Again.

It turned out that the oil pressure gauge pipe had decided to leak, and I'm ashamed to say it got to March before I asked Kelvin to have a look.

Quest was no more as Sunny had retired, but Kelvin had kept a classic car-friendly face in place by starting his own business, Fusion Autocraft. Annoyingly for my mum, but perhaps happily for Kelvin, my mum's Midget was also undriveable at the time because the clutch master cylinder had decided to part with its seal, sending fluid all over the driver's footwell and rendering the clutch useless. Luckily, parts are readily available for the Midget, and the MG Owners' Club provided a new master cylinder for a total of £75.82 including delivery, and Kelvin towed both cars back to the workshop to work on them at the same time.

Maggie's problem was a leak in the oil line going to the oil pressure gauge. This is basically a pipe going from the engine block to the back of the dash, and the pressure in that moves the needle on the gauge, in very simple terms. Another example of genius '50s engineering — when it works.

Both jobs, including a new battery for the Midget, which was needed as the cheap one I'd sourced wasn't holding charge, came to £335 and we were up and running again. It was a double bonus for me as I had an excuse to drive the Midget the short distance from Orrell to my mum's before cadging a lift back with my mum in her modern car for the Magnette. It may have been the very last day of March, but a very, very light flutter of snow on the short drive home made me more than a little bit nervous considering I had drum brakes all round. But we were back in business, albeit three months after the problem revealed itself.

The start of the show season came and went. Drive It Day — a day in April where classic car owners are encouraged to go out and enjoy their vehicles as a kind of nationwide 'show' — came and went. And I'm sheepish to admit all I used Maggie for was the odd trip to the butcher's and pootle around the block. I was a very bad custodian of the ZA.

So Gary decided to intervene. The seven months to August 2022 had flown by in the whirlwind of work, writing this book and raising a nearly two-year-old. So he told me I was going to the Town Show at Newton le Willows, a town in Merseyside, not far from me down the East Lancashire Road. In Maggie. He'd already registered me as a guest of his club.

This, and nice weather, put a spring in my step ahead of the date on 6th August. I checked and inflated my tyres, topped the ZA up with fresh fuel and tweaked the ignition timing as it was running a little quick. You do this by fiddling with a couple of screws near the carburettor fuel chambers I was now so familiar with and listening for the right note. As a musician with near perfect pitch — an ability to tell the note being played by listening to it — I like to think I'm half decent at getting the timing right.

A few days' driving around the village boosted my confidence and gave the car a much-needed run in the wild. Seeing it in places like the Co-op car park and putting actual shopping in the boot, hearing the wine bottle clink with each gentle bump on the way home was what I imagined through those dark winters of restoration.

We were all set.

A sticky throttle on the way to the show was fixed with a few mashes of the pedal and a few shakes of the linkage under the bonnet, and joining the small convoy through the streets felt incredible. I was even more proud to have left the car's appearance in its battle-scarred state when I was complimented on it numerous times. I've said before that I want my car to wear its history.

A Spitfire flyover gave me goosebumps, and being the one in a camping chair and not asking people to move them out of shot while cajoling them for interviews was a nice change. Camping chairs are a no-no when taking pictures for publication, they just look messy.

My day was made even better when Sophie arrived with our son, spending the afternoon clambering in and out of our cars and managing to get in the cab of his dream ride — a John Deere tractor. Getting him out of the tractor was a hard task, and the promise of letting him sit in a '*nee nor*' (that's a fire engine to you) got him away from the agricultural vehicles, but presented a new problem in how to get him out of the nee nor. I'm just glad he's so passionate about what he likes.

My drive home was alone as the disadvantage of classic motoring is a lack of isofix (and that's not the only reason, any child of mine is going nowhere near a classic car until they are old enough to assess the risk for themselves). But it left me with thoughts of my late dad and how pleased he'd have been. Nothing, it seemed, could dent my mood as I took in friendly paps and waves from other motorists on the East Lancashire Road. We did it, dad, I thought. It was hard, long, fraught with frustration and I was downright irresponsible in throwing money that was begged for, inherited and credit carded after a project which was self-indulgent and brimming with grief. I've said repeatedly since that I don't think I should have done it, but Sophie reassured me that I'd regret it more if I hadn't done it. I can't help thinking where the money would be now if we hadn't done the car, but then again, I was always going to do the car, so is there any point wondering?

Bikers, a few fellow classic drivers and the odd occupant of a modern car parped or waves as I trundled home down the East Lancs and back up to Billinge. The scenery, including the woods and the view of the beacon, my lifelong thinking place and where I proposed to Sophie, made me feel grateful to be in this part of the world. The no-man's land between Wigan and St Helens and one of the most beautiful places on Earth. Not necessarily because of the scenery — that would belong to the Scottish Highlands — but because of what it means to me and a few thousand other people. And it isn't too shabby to look at either.

My joy was short-lived, though. I decided to go out again the following day to find a puddle of oil coming from the back of the offside back wheel.

Keeper of Magnette parts Peter Martin sorted me out with a new wheel cylinder for £36, and Kelvin was called into action again.

This time, I didn't wait three months. I asked him to give the car a once over and service while he fixed the leak. The latest bill of £410 for the seals to be replaced, along with an oil and coolant change, grease points serviced and a clean of the rear wheel bearing included new materials and giving the car a check.

By this point he had moved his business from Orrell to Skelmersdale, making my five-minute drive to his garage a 12-minute one, but I enjoyed it immensely. By now, with lots of use, Maggie was starting on the button — Kelvin even said it was the fastest starting classic car he knew — and it morphed into a different car when it was running up to temperature. It wasn't clunky, I was more confident, and it felt like mine at last, as much as I wanted my dad to be there to see it.

Kelvin recommended getting the sills and box sections cavity waxed to ward off, or at least slow down, future problems as we'd seen so much welding go into the car, and my plans for the spring were to address some minor leaks. In the meantime, I promised to drive it. As much as possible.

24

The Past

Ferrari Testarossa Spider
I'm claiming this as the first car I ever drove — on the Sega Master System. Out Run was released in 1986, and we got our Master System in about 1991, so I'd have been four. I still haven't completed the drive to the goal line, even though it only takes five minutes, and I remember being incensed when my older brother managed the feat while sitting in front of the television on the cream carpet.

One day, in 2016, I was clicking away at my desk drawing-up a sports page for the *Wigan Post* when my editor's phone rang on the desk next to me. Nothing unusual there.

When Phil Wilkinson (said editor) then patched the call through to me, there was also nothing unusual about that, calls got passed around quite a bit. The unusual part was instead of this being a call from a parent wanting to tell me about a rugby try-scoring feat by their offspring for the paper, this person wanted to talk about my car.

Not wanting to draw attention to myself while taking what had become a personal call in the newsroom, I was vague on the phone while I listened to a man called Andrew Gosling tell me he had a connection with Maggie. One evening, he did what a lot of car enthusiasts did and Googled the reg number to see if it was still 'alive' on the DVLA website. At the time he'd have got a shock, as the website showed it hadn't been on the road since 1984, but a bit of further Googling led Andrew to *Classic Car Weekly*, where I had just started writing updates on the Magnette's restoration.

'Can I take your number and call you back?'

I wrote it down on a notepad, genuinely excited that a previous owner of my car had found me. I couldn't wait to have a conversation about what the car was like in a past life, what work might have been done to it, and pick through memories to go with mine and my dad's car. I kept the number in the notepad and folded the page face up, then placed the notepad with the Magnette's paperwork and didn't call the number for six years.

It was November 2022, when in the final stages of writing this book, that I finally made the call. By now, the page on the notepad seemed toilet-paper thin and the ink was faded, and I don't know why I left it so long to make the call. There wasn't an answer, then after five minutes, Andrew called back.

It wasn't that the car belonged to him, Andrew explained, but he became associated with it by marriage. It was his wife, Margaret I wanted to speak to, so we arranged for me to call a couple of days later.

It turns out Maggie was the first car Margaret drove, in 1964. She was a teenager as she sat behind the steering wheel for the first time.

'We were by our house and my mother told me how to do everything but steer it, and I went up the kerb,' she said, as I strained to hear thanks to the bad phone signal in my house. Unlike my first experience driving the Magnette, Margaret wasn't left doubting her ability as a driver.

'I didn't have a problem because it was the first car I drove. It had good acceleration.'

Margaret and Andrew had owned the car until 1972, when my records begin. My big box file of papers from the restoration started as a single folded brown envelope with 'Z.A. SLC. 620' written on it in my dad's writing. There's the receipt I mentioned earlier on, and a small pile of loose paper, the oldest being the old style green registration book with which some of this book's older readers will be familiar. It was registered with Nottinghamshire County Council.

'That's right,' Margaret explained. 'I was offered a job where I would be travelling from Nottingham to Loughbrough every day, and that's when I knew I'd have to part with it.'

By then Maggie was 16 years old, and already a 'bit of a collector's item' according to Margaret. It was around this time a lot of Magnettes were meeting their end. The Who's *Quadrophenia*, released in 1973, features a picture of a ZB getting its window smashed, then being flipped on its roof in the album insert.

But luckily, no such fate was awaiting Maggie.

'We spent quite a bit of money getting it looking decent,' she said, also explaining it was under her ownership the engine was swapped from the original to a goldseal replacement after it let her down on a drive home, and it had new sills, not for the only time in its life.

'It was the family car, and my parents weren't doing much with it. My father died in 1969, and my mother decided to get a smaller car, so I had the Magnette.'

Like the ZA played its part at my parents' wedding, it went on honeymoon with Andrew and Margaret to the Lake District, after it became their only car in 1970, before they sold it in 1972.

'The man who came to buy it came round in a ZB, he was buying it for his dad,' said Margaret. 'We sold it in May, I had nearly reached the end of my student days and got a job in Loughborough to start a little later in the year. At this point we realised it wasn't going to be practical to keep the MG as it was increasingly difficult to get parts and I needed a reliable car. We had to wait three months for an exhaust and we had to have a speedo cable made for us when that broke. Reluctantly we sold it for around £150. For comparison, Andrew's father bought a new car around this time for about £700 — it just shows how prices for everything have rocketed since then. We were aware that these cars were becoming a collectors item by then.'

In talking about the big file and where my history starts, Margaret also helped by providing a timeline for the period SLC 620 was in her family.

Her dad, TE Banks, bought it in the summer of 1960 from a garage in Epsom, Surrey, and Margaret told me all the admin was in his name, despite the fact she can't remember him driving a car though he had a licence at one time.

'It was taken almost straight away on holiday to Scotland,' she said. 'Then I first drove the car in the early summer of 1964, on obtaining my provisional licence and did much of my learning in it. My father died in 1969 and so the car would then have been registered, in Ashtead, in my mother's name IP Banks, then in late 1969 or early 1970, probably around Christmas or New Year, when I was at home, the car was transferred to me as my mother decided to get a smaller car.

'At that time we were aware that the engine was not in good health and so I wasn't expecting I would have the car for long. It would have been registered in my name, which was then MH Banks. I was a postgraduate student at Nottingham University at the time.'

Margaret left the car in Newcastle in the summer of 1970 when she went to Iceland for three months on an expedition from Newcastle upon Tyne University. She trusted a friend to look after it, and it was when she was driving back to Nottingham in late September the original engine finally gave up, somewhere near Northallerton.

'I was able to get it to a garage and at that point it was either replace the engine or scrap the car,' she said.

'I chose the former and a reconditioned engine was fitted.'
After meeting Andrew later that year, Margaret explained that 'some TLC' was needed to get the car into better shape, before their honeymoon, and they continued to look after it.

'We kept the car in good condition, work being carried out by a back street garage in Sandiacre,' she said.

'The owners charged very reasonable prices to students [Andrew was also a postgraduate student] but were also very capable and good with bodywork. Andrew found the car hard to drive at first as he had been used to a more modern vehicle — he commented that the gear stick seemed very long.'

When Margaret sold the ZA, it cost the new buyer, who lived in Beeston, £25 for a year's tax. Five years later, the vehicle was transferred from its male owner to a female of the same surname at the same address. I can only speculate it went sideways to his wife seeing as it was already bought for him by his son, possibly ruling out him passing it down to a daughter to learn in.

By 1973, Maggie had covered 87,785 of the 112,000 or so it has done today — unless it has been around the clock again, but I very much doubt it managed more than 100,000 miles in the ten years before it was garaged for the next 30, so I think 112,000 is a safe bet. In October 1973, the owner paid £8.73 for a new front brake cylinder and the brakes being bled, at a garage in Toton which seems to have closed in around 2001. The same company did an MOT in 1972 with a change of engine oil and filter for £4.30, and the next two MOTs, for 1973 and '74 were £1.70 each. There was a repair to an 'under body panel' — worryingly a month after its 1973 MOT — for £3, then there's nothing for 1975 until an MOT certificate for 1976, with the owner moving services to a garage aptly-named the Magnet Garage in Long Eaton, a very short drive to Toton. The Magnet Garage still exists in the same place, as Long Eaton Garage Services, and you can see pictures of the garage in the 1920s on the Sawley and District Historical Society website. There's also an invoice for £21.32 from October 1978, a week after its MOT, which indicates some slightly more serious work needed to be done as only five years before you could get a panel repaired for £3. This time it had an 'MOT Test Repair a/r' and I can't decide what that repair might be, some new seals in the left hand front brake and a new exhaust system which was £6.75. (For comparison, a new exhaust system in 2019 was £278.82 and I got a discount to £250.94 because I was spending £1798.20 on parts in a single order at the time).

Then it was sold on 24th June, 1979.

I wonder about the state of the car in 1978 because not only was there that big invoice (by the standards of the others in the envelope from the time), but the owner did roughly 2,000 miles a year in the Magnette until the MOT ran out in October 1977, then it wasn't renewed for a year and only 28 miles were added to the clock. Was the car in need of a rebuild at this point or had a few niggles led the owner to lose patience? I'll probably never know. He got £375 for the car and the handwritten invoice is signed by someone who was not the owner at the 1978 MOT.

This confuses me, because V5C certificates used to say how many former keepers a car had on the front cover, and when I got the logbook in my name, the figure was four.

For those keeping track, we're already over this number by 1979. We have: The original owner from 1956 to 1960 — assuming there is only one.

Margaret Gosling's parents from 1960 to 1969.

Margaret Gosling from 1969 to 1972.

W Otley from 1972 to 1977.

F Otely from 1977 to what I'd assume is at least 1978, as the £21 mega invoice is made-out to an I Otley.

On blue paper, the invoice reads: Car is accepted in condition as seen, tried and tested. Current MOT and road tax are in force at time of sale.

Following this, my dad's friend bought it in 1981, so for sake of ease let's assume there's no one else in-between the 1979 sale and him. I don't have an invoice for him, but I do have a letter written to him from the MG Owner's Club dated 24th February, 1981 advising him a Magnette would be a good fit. He obviously moved quickly, because there's only 11 days from the date of this letter and the date he sold Maggie to my dad.

The friend whose wife didn't like the car, a man named Geoff Martin, takes-up his version of the story, which isn't far from what my dad used to tell us.

'I went down to Nottingham to pick it up,' he said. 'On the drive back I realised it needed some things doing, but loved it.

'But my wife at the time was not very keen and I only had it for about three weeks. Selling it to your dad was very, very quick. I fell in love with it and your dad fell in love with it.

'It was in the garage where I lived in St Helens for about two weeks and my ex-wife decided she didn't like it and your dad came and said, "Well I'll buy it off you."

'It would have been a lovely car for me but the powers that be were against it.'

Then there was me. I make myself at least the ninth owner. The tenth if you included my dad's dad for the month between the sale and my dad's birthday.

It was, I'm guessing by early 1980s standards, an expensive February for my dad in 1982, almost a year after he'd been given the car. A teacher, he might not have been earning far off the average wage of £154 per week, so he'd spent almost a week's wage on a couple of familiar items and two that don't burden me as Maggie's custodian.

It had an exhaust at £32.14, which didn't last long considering the last one was only three years before (and does that explain why the last one was so cheap?) and my dad had also bought a starter motor for £20.53. These cost £76.94 when I thought I needed one. He'd also spent £47.12 on the MOT, suggesting it needed work as an MOT is roughly that today, and £38.50 on tax, which is free for historic vehicles now. He got his money's worth though, and was putting miles on the car, taking it to work (he told me a story of the head teacher asking which member of staff had come to work in a police car — Z types had at one time been used as police cars, along with the similar-looking Wolsleys).

The MOT expired in December 1981, and in 1980 it had covered 99,905 miles by the time it went on the tester's ramp. My dad took a break in '81, waiting until March 1982 to put it through its next MOT (probably because of the money that needed spending) and by then it had gone round the clock, the odometer showing 3,174 miles. By 1983 that was up to 7,107 miles, it's last MOT for more than 30 years, and I know he did similar mileage before the car took its place in the garage to pose as a taxi because the clock showed 12,000 miles throughout my childhood.

In that time, it was a wedding car to a couple of my parents' friends in the MG Owners' Club, and then theirs in 1983. It was such a short time on the road, so why go through all that aggro to put it back there 30 years later?

'Because he loved that car,' my mum said, long after we'd finished the project. It was December, 2022, and I'd had the file out again, going through the car's history, or as much of it as I have before I increased the size of the file tenfold with bills and orders for parts.

We'd nipped out for a coffee, and talk of the car means talk of my dad, which is easier now than it was a few years ago, but it still caused her to put her teapot down and concentrate on what she was saying.

'I was in a pub with my then-boyfriend when I first saw Maggie,' she explained as we both warmed our hands on our cups. It was cold enough to make my fingers numb enough to mean recording our chat on my phone was more of a faff than usual. Plates clinked and coffee grinders whirred to provide the usual backing track to most of the interviews I've ever recorded. With

100 words-per-minute I'd like to say the majority are in shorthand notebooks, but the reality is different.

'Your dad came into the pub and said, "Do you want to come and look at my new MG?" to my boyfriend, because he liked cars.

'We all went out and had a look at it and I thought "it's very big for a sports car," because I thought all MGs were sports cars. When I split-up with said boyfriend of the time, your dad worked at Edmund Campion [a school in St Helens] which was right by my parents' house, and he used to drive past it all the time. One day I was washing my Spitfire and he stopped in the Magnette and he got out and we had a chat."

This, by the way, backs-up my dad's story about how he met my mum. I've never asked mum until now, but dad always used to simply say: 'I chatted her up.'

Anyway, mum was speaking, and I'd just asked her what Maggie was like to drive.

'I only drove it once. Around the block, from Leahurst (that was my dad's parents' house) and it was lovely. I remember thinking how easy it was to drive considering it was so big. It's small, now, but then it was like driving a bus.'

So what happened? I really wanted to know how it ended-up in a garage for more than 30 years if it was loved so much.

'We just didn't have the time, and we didn't have the money,' my mum said. 'We just didn't have any spare money... at all. We were living in a house that was way above our means and we struggled; we really did struggle.'

They may have struggled, but I'm grateful my parents did a good job of hiding it from us.

And while my dad wasn't able to bring Maggie out of hibernation, my brother and I were able to try and get our Ferrari Testarossa Spider to the goal line.

25

The Future

DMC DeLorean

Looking at what is in store for me and Maggie, there's only really one choice — specifically Doc Brown's DMC DeLorean. While the DeLorean Motor Company failed miserably, with poor quality, poor performance, poor sales and a tale of a company tangled in scandal, their desirability has persevered. People's love of crap cars, 1980s chic and Back to the Future *has undoubtedly helped. I've just Googled 'DeLorens for sale' and seen prices north of £40,000.*

On 21st November, 2014, my dad had been dead for nine months and I had just turned 27. I hadn't a clue about cars, other than I rather liked old ones.

Raw grief was still coarsing through my veins.

I had known Sophie for about two years and we were happy, apart from the times my grief reared its head, and we rented a tiny, but beautiful, two bedroomed cottage. It was just us.

On 7th September 2020, my dad had been dead for six-and-a-half years and I was approaching my 33rd birthday. I hadn't a clue about cars, other than I rather liked old ones, and I'd now driven a few of them. Weathered, sometimes rough, sometimes comforting, grief was on a hook like an old coat. I sometimes put it on. Sophie and I had been married for 13 months and two weeks and we were happy. It was the due date for our first child and we owned a nice house which is bigger than the cottage but doesn't have as much character. It was us, Otis, and our bump.

That was the day I first drove Maggie. For three miles.

It was 2,117 days from the day the Magnette's logbook arrived in my name to the first time I drove it.

Writing this book has been as much therapy as restoring the car. Less expensive, but I couldn't have written about it had I not done it. I just totted-up the total. That's not entirely true, I already knew roughly what the total is.

Many people helped finance my indulgence, and there were times they didn't really have a choice given the stage the project was in, or their own emotional investment in it — and me. My mum could, and probably should, have said no. My siblings have a right to be furious. My student loan should have been smaller. My inheritance should have chipped into the mortgage.

In all, if you include parts, the total bill has topped £30,000. For a car which I could maybe sell for £8,000 on a good day. Some would say half that.

Which begs the question: Why?

And why me? I'll let my mum explain.

'I never really thought any of you would be that interested (in taking the car on when my dad died).

'I decided I couldn't do it, which one of you would care because I really didn't want to part with it because your dad adored that car.

'I did what I did to keep your dad's memory alive.'

Even hearing that, I didn't feel any guilt wash away for the cap-in-hand moments, despite my mum's best efforts to reassure me.

'It had to be done,' she said with a matter-of-fact expression.

'We'd gone too far. Let's finish it. You can't half-do a project and then let it go. I didn't want your dad to sell his Midget, that was a bone of contention, for me. He let me drive that Midget to work and we were a couple, but we weren't like, a stamped-on couple, and an ex-girlfriend saw me drive that car and was really upset.'

Hearing this made me remember the day I found said Midget for sale, and I remember pacing my lounge as the seller read out the registration to me.

'I spoke to your grandad about it,' my mum said.

'He said "leave it where it is".'

Back to the Magnette, it was never about what the car was worth or might be worth. To me, my Magnette is a spectacular car. To a classic car connoisseur, it really isn't. It's not even ordinary if you consider the condition it is still in. Yes, it has been welded to the ends of the earth and is a solid little bus now, but the paintwork is scuffed, the chrome is pitted and the leather is torn. I want it that way. There's a cigarette end in one of the ashtrays that either belongs to my dad or my grandma. There's a ring pull from a can of pop from the '80s. I know this because the design is different and I looked it up. And it has to be, no one has drunk a can of pop in it since then, it's been in the garage.

There's a receipt for tyres in the glovebox, put there by my dad. And a box of matches.

Then there's my small mark on the car. A scratch on new paint from trying to squeeze my lawnmower past it in the garage and the indicator switches under the steering column because fixing the original, which is still in place, was too expensive. Could the whole thing be summed-up in a sentence? It's a grief project. Or at least that's why I spent so much time, effort and money on this one, instead of spending a third of the final figure on a mint condition one that wasn't once my dad's.

But I also felt like I was saving something. History — the big stuff — is important, you'd hope that's how we learn despite the efforts of those in power (and many who are not) to convince us otherwise. But the not so important stuff, like keeping old cars going, is fascinating. I get almost as excited when I open a cupboard and find a magazine that has been untouched for 50 years, or a decades-old carpet in a house which reveals what it looked like when it was new when the sideboard is pushed away from the wall. There was an easter egg on a shelf at my grandad's house from when my dad was a toddler. It was from Thornton's and had 'William' written on it. The box had an illustration with ducklings and 'ABC, 123' on the sides. Inside was a perfectly-preserved Easter egg. The conditions in my grandad's extension above the garage (he was stingy with the heating) must have been perfect. I was obsessed with it. It was from about 1958 and it was 35 years old when I first became aware of it. When he died and we were clearing out his house I'd have kept everything if I had my own way — so would my sister. Carrier bags from long-gone shops, records in paper bags, car parts still boxed-up. A lot of the time the items were packaged with seals unbroken. There was just too much of it. It's the mundane side of history I enjoy. I don't necessarily care about kings and queens, I want to know what Joe Bloggs who shopped in St Helens in the '50s thought of the new-ish National Health Service and whether he thought he'd 'never had it so good.'

What did he drive, where did his kids go to school, what did he eat, what beer did he drink in the pub — was there a choice? As well as the ties to my dad, saving this car will, hopefully, also save a small piece of this history.

But to what extent?

The most obvious obstacle to Maggie's future, in the car's current guise, is the fact it runs on fossil fuels. I've read countless tweets and opinions on the carbon footprint of a classic car, and classic car insurer Footman James's 2022 Indicator Report suggests classic cars' impact on the environment is less than new cars, though it depends how you look at the data (and, as a journalist, I think it's important to note where it has come from).

But it makes for interesting reading.

The report says a classic car, travelling a yearly average of 1,200 miles, generates 563kg of CO_2 per year, when a modern emits up to 6.8 tonnes of CO_2 before it even departs the factory, as in, that is what the carbon cost of the production process is. Footman James states: 'The in-depth research study also states that even though a modern car would, in fact, be more efficient and use less fuel if used on a daily basis, the environmental cost of manufacturing a new vehicle immediately negates this.'

The report went further, stating one type of electric car is 'said to' create 26 tonnes of CO_2 during the production process, a figure which would take a typical classic car 46 years to match.

That may seem ok, but it doesn't take into account that we're talking a very big range to find the 'average' classic car. A V12 muscle car would be very different to a Metro, for example. The 'said to' line is also ambiguous when talking about electric cars.

And I'm not saying I dispute the claims. I'm obviously very much in the 'classic cars are ace' camp, and I have my doubts about how efficient electric vehicles are when the environmental cost of producing them is totted-up — It's one of the reasons I kept my 13-year-old Insignia until it died. I just don't know what the right thing is to do, and I have a hunch it's environmentally kinder to run that into the ground than to get a new car every year.

But I'm also worried — and not about having orange paint thrown over the Magnette. I question, even if the Indicator Report is right, if burning any amount of petrol is acceptable. Should I have done the restoration at all? I wanted to preserve history, but at what cost?

Is synthetic fuel the answer to our hobby? Dominic Taylor-Lane of the Associateion of Heritage Engineers describes such a case in the foreword to this book. Would I consider converting the Magnette to electric power? There are services which take the batteries from written-off electric cars and convert classics to run on them. We could also argue about the production of the battery and the carbon cost of that. Does that ruin a car's classic status? Well, not if you go off what I said about upgrades had the car been on the road its whole life. Will I even have a choice? As it stands, sales of all new petrol and diesel cars will end in the UK in 2030, and who knows if and when sales of petrol and diesel to fuel old cars will stop?

There are more questions than answers as Maggie begins the next phase of its life, and its future is at its most uncertain. When I was young, the only question was if it would ever see the road again, but no one was questioning whether it should — there was hardly any social focus at all. It was just interesting. And with all the questions about types of fuel, do we go electric? And what is the cost of running a classic car? I think, as much as I love cars, that the answer to one of the many problems we face is our relationship with them.

I know there are thousands of strands to the environmental challenges we face, but the most obvious answer to the impact our own transport has on the planet is to accept a big change. We shouldn't be using cars every day. And that's impossible for many as it stands. For me to get the train to work would cost me £50 per month more than fuel and parking does. They are cancelled frequently and the earliest train I can walk to from home doesn't get me to work on time. But has the Covid pandemic taught us that we can rethink how we work and travel less? Would more people be willing to use their cars less if trains were affordable and reliable?

The role Maggie plays in all of this is small.

She has so far covered a lot less than the 1,200 miles per year that the Indicator Report states is average and would never be pressed into daily use, but I wonder what my children will make of her when they are the age I was when I was being asked if there was a taxi in my garage. By early 2023, Maggie was stuck in my garage with the same problem as 12 months before. Just like when I started writing this book as a student at the university library in 2019, the car was undriveable.

Unlike 2019, I now had a sleeping toddler next to me as I typed and we were expecting our second baby too.

Since Kelvin repaired the car after the show I had barely used it. It hadn't been out for ages and that was absolutely my fault. I had no excuse for not starting it up and at least driving around the block. The last time I tried to start it, after many unsuccessful attempts I'd ended-up with just the clicking sound the starter motor made before I called on Gary to help. I'll be doing that again soon and he assures me we will get it started.

But I worry.

I have wondered about selling Maggie, now that the project is out of my system, to give myself less to worry about and more space in the garage, but Sophie, and I think rightly, reckons I will come to regret that when our children are old enough for me not to be in their immediate vicinity at all times to ensure their survival. Sure, weekends will always be about family time, swimming and whatever they want to do, but there will be rain-free evenings where there will be an hour to tinker in the garage and go for a drive. There will be shows, and they may even take an interest and want to be included.

They won't be forced, though. I want to treat my children as I was treated and find their own way with their interests. It is also blindingly obvious when I do think about selling it, that this isn't my car to sell, even if I wanted to — which I don't.

For Maggie, ideally I would like to think there's an answer down the line in synthetic fuels, though I would be willing to explore the electric conversion offer if it becomes apparent that would be the only way to preserve the car for longer. You can explore all the reasons I've talked about from my dad's memory to preserving history for wanting to keep the Magnette running, and my children, though they aren't going to be forced, will have the option to continue that after me if they want to.

Some may also pass judgement on my custodianship of the car, as is natural, and some will think it's great I oversaw people more capable than I am bring it back from the dead while others will think it would be better off in the hands of an expert with more time to devote to it than I have at the moment.

My position is I believe you can like cars, and old cars, and drive them and own them without being an expert. We don't all possess the technical abilities of Juan Manuel Fangio and we may even crunch the odd gear and not know how to fix more than a simple problem, but people in this bracket, who like cars for a range of reasons, from seeing them pop-up in cultural references to wanting what their parents had, should all be allowed their space in this hobby. People should also be allowed to maintain, upgrade and modify their own cars as they please, as long as it's safe. You might not put a nodding dog on the dashboard of a Silver Ghost, but if it's your car and you want the nodding dog, then go for it.

The feeling I get when I drive Maggie will be the same as countless other enthusiasts when they drive their own cars. And the feeling I get when I fix a problem will be shared. There are other people who own cars that once belonged to dead parents, or friends, and these serve the same purpose in honouring that person and providing comfort to the one left behind, even if the car causes grief by breaking down or denting the new owner's head when they stand up from being under the bonnet. I know what I believe and I know what makes me feel better, and they are not the same thing, so I like to think my dad knows the car is back on the road and I like to think he's in the passenger seat from time to time because I can't accept he's not. And that's what drove me to see this through.

That's why it had to be *this* car.

26

Afterword

Keeway X-Light 125
I wanted this to say 'Royal Enfield Classic 350' or 'Royal Enfield Bullet 500', but I keep putting my foot down on my test so I have to make do with a 125 and L-Plates, for now at least. The Keeyway looks quite nice and there are certainly worse bikes to own, and being on two wheels has given me a new-found respect for those who get around this way. More importantly, the Magnette is back in good health.

Since the rodent-induced hiatus of winter 2023, the Magnette has indeed been brought back to life – again – by Kel and a friend of Gary Brunskill, who has devoted countless hours to my cause. His name is Bill Parr and he is a retired mechanic.

After more than half a year of inactivity with my ZA not starting, it took Kel three days to fix it and have it back to me.

I've spent too much time beating myself up for not looking after Maggie, when all I needed to do was ask for help earlier, much earlier.

After I failed to solve the starting issue with a new starter solenoid, unwelcome visitors made their way into my garage and into the boot of the Magnette, and evidence under the bonnet suggested they'd used my wiring loom as a snack, which added to my woes, and the latest episode made me wonder whether I'm the best person to look after this car, a familiar feeling.

Bill, a Sunbeam Rapier owner and member of the Phoenix Classic Vehicle Association of St Helens spent most of the summer of 2023 poring over Maggie with Gary while I welcomed my second-born son into the world.

The idea was that they got to play cars and when I get to join in I won't have to start again after weeks (or months) of inactivity with Fionn joining William in the family. He came with all the same worry and all the same joy, and the house is as chaotic as you'd think with me and two boys in it. Sophie has super powers.

Kel got the car started again with a new battery and he also traced all the wiring to assess the extent of the damage caused by mice. Luckily, he could only find one small section of chewed casing in the bulkhead area, so he fixed that as well as cleaning the connections, and he fitted a new earth strap while he was there.

As the car was with him, Kel also replaced the offside rear driveshaft hubseal, a recommendation he made when he did the nearside the summer before.

When Kel called to say the car was ready I was more than a little relieved. Asking Sophie for a lift, the drive back home was a joy, for the first ten minutes.

A job I hadn't attended to properly is the wire that goes into the back of the temperature gauge. It was just sort of twisted round and scrunched in because I hadn't bothered to find a bullet connector that actually fits. I didn't know this at the time, but as I approached the first roundabout (and in Skelmersdale there are many) my fuel gauge just dropped. I was nervous anyway because the fuel in the car was old, and when the gauge dropped from just over a quarter to empty, with most of my journey home to go, I was in squeaky-bum mode. It didn't register with me at the time, but the fact the indicators also stopped working at the same time should have been a sign.

With clenched teeth and prayers I trundled home, going past the petrol station en route as it only sells E10. I'd never been more relieved to get home.

Of course you'll know, and Gary knew, and Bill knew, that the fuel gauge and indicator issue was because of a blown fuse, caused by the temperature gauge wire popping out and touching something. Sure enough, I had plenty of fuel to get home.

From there Bill and Gary spent most Wednesdays fettling with, and improving, the car and eventually overhauled the carburettors and adjusted the timing. Maggie runs like a dream and has been used little and often despite me giving in to my long-standing desire to learn to ride a motorbike.

It's fun, but it's not got quite the same attraction as Maggie.

Mum and dad

Acknowledgements

You need a special group of capable and understanding people around you to look after a classic car – and you need a special group of capable and understanding people around you when you decide to write about cars.

Sophie, thank you – not just for being the heartbeat of this wonderful chaotic house and for our sons, but for putting up with my taste for old things that don't work properly. As a writer, it is a frustrating source of embarrassment that I can't find the words to tell you how much I love you.

Mum, thank you not just for help when things got mega-tough, for childcare and pep-talks, but all the little stuff that seemingly goes unnoticed. It doesn't, and I will fix the shelf soon.

Gary and Bill, without your knowledge I'd be truly stuck. Your generosity and willingness to take payment in hot drinks for the hours of effort you have put into the car is genuinely humbling.

Phil Caplan and Tony Hannan. Thank you for believing in this project, and for helping me to realise another dream.

Tom and Maggie

Also from Scratching Shed

DRIVING THE REAL GREAT NORTH ROAD

ANDY BULL

Join travel writer Andy Bull as he drives – and tells the story of – the original 400-mile route from London to Edinburgh via the UK's very own version of 'Route 66'

Visit www.scratchingshedpublishing.com

Investigate our other titles and
stay up to date with all our latest releases at
www.scratchingshedpublishing.co.uk